Becoming a Peaceful Powered Leader

Endorsements for
Becoming a Peaceful Powered Leader

Becoming A Peaceful Powered Leader is filled with powerful growth opportunities and insights for leaders and organizations alike. Narlock's approach to understanding and defining purpose and success—coupled with a truly hands-on approach to leveraging emotional intelligence—is a game changer for leaders and organizations looking to take their skills and performance to the next level. He backs it with research and a real-world, practical approach to accountability and goals that both inspires and elevates you to be your best—and to own your peace.

—**Christopher D. Connors**, Bestselling Author of *Emotional Intelligence for the Modern Leader* and *Keynote Speaker*

A big part of my leadership approach has centered on self-awareness and coachability. In *Becoming a Peaceful Powered Leader*, Jared Narlock drives this concept home. Only when we can recognize the fear and ego that drives us can we break old patterns and lead from a more centered place. Not only does this create a sense of inner peace, but it also frees us to engage people in the deep, meaningful way needed to power the workplace of the future. And it creates a more humanistic company—one that attracts the best employees and creates the healthy relationships needed to collaborate at a high level and solve problems. This book shifts how you see things, so you start reacting differently… and gives you the tools and tactics to make the change sustainable.

—**Quint Studer**, Author of *The Calling: Why Healthcare is So Special*

The world needs more Peaceful Powered Leaders. It needs folks that are willing to be vulnerable and truthful, willing to share failures and make it okay for others to do the same. This book is a wonderful guide to take yourself on the journey to becoming a leader who goes beyond inspiring and changes lives. Don't just read it, live it.

—**April Shprintz**, Creator of The Generosity Culture® and Author of *Magic Blue Rocks - The Secret to Doing Anything*

There are countless resources on leadership and it's hard to break through with something 'new' and relevant, but Jared Narlock does just this. He reframes leadership in a way that makes it more tangible, others focused AND relevant !! Being a peaceful leader in a time when everything seems to be uncertain and unknown is on point. I plan to use the learnings I've gleaned from his good work and put it to use personally in my life and in my role in my company. Lead with, and through, peace !!

—**Steve Browne**, SHRM-SCP, Chief People Officer of LaRosa's, Inc. and Author of *HR on Purpose!!* and *HR Rising!!*

A practical and inspiring guide to help you lead with authenticity and accountability—and be a force of good in the lives of others.

—**Nataly Kogan**, Author of *Happier Now*

Jared puts himself in the shoes of the leader, and shows how to lead a life of intention, service, and care with a beautiful guide for how to show up for the most important people in your life—at home and in the workplace.

—**Bryan Wish**, Chief Executive Officer of BW Missions

Becoming a Peaceful POWERED LEADER

How to Shed Fear, Live Courageously, and Own Your Peace

Jared Narlock

NEW YORK

LONDON • NASHVILLE • MELBOURNE • VANCOUVER

Becoming a Peaceful Powered Leader

How to Shed Fear, Live Courageously, and Own Your Peace

Published in New York, New York, by Morgan James Publishing. Morgan James is a trademark of Morgan James, LLC. www.MorganJamesPublishing.com

Morgan James BOGO™

A **FREE** ebook edition is available for you or a friend with the purchase of this print book.

CLEARLY SIGN YOUR NAME ABOVE

Instructions to claim your free ebook edition:
1. Visit MorganJamesBOGO.com
2. Sign your name CLEARLY in the space above
3. Complete the form and submit a photo of this entire page
4. You or your friend can download the ebook to your preferred device

ISBN 9781631955334 paperback
ISBN 9781631955341 ebook
Library of Congress Control Number:
2021935177

Cover and Interior Design by:
Chris Treccani
www.3dogcreative.net

Morgan James is a proud partner of Habitat for Humanity Peninsula and Greater Williamsburg. Partners in building since 2006.

Get involved today! Visit
MorganJamesPublishing.com/giving-back

This book is dedicated to the leaders who are striving daily to create a humanistic and authentic approach to leadership. Those who connect optimism to action with a vision of a workplace that has the heart, vulnerability, and trust that other areas of our lives consist of and bring forward. Those loyal to leading with peace in a powerful way, in service to others. Thank you all! It is not easy, but I know so many humans truly appreciate it.

Contents

Foreword

"Originally, the word power meant able to be.
In time, it was contracted to mean to be able.
We suffer the difference."
Mark Nepo

Leadership is the immediate provision of power over resources, people, and teams with a single act: the granting of a title. Most leaders find themselves promoted as a result of their abilities or knowledge—their ableness in the external world. It is their skills and mastery of the external environment that earned them their position, but it won't earn them their place in the world or in the hearts of those they lead.

The very thing they will need to be successful leaders isn't mastery of the external landscape but mastery of the mysterious inner scape, their ability to be. Unfortunately, the very power granted to them gives them disincentive to go within, reflect, get vulnerable, and tend to their own evolution so that they can move about the world not only skillfully but lovingly as well. Instead, it reenforces the illusion that they can succeed by intellectually figuring out strategies and techniques to influence others to create great results. This is the perfect condition for the ego to thrive and build up all the false identities and resulting behaviors we see so rampant in leadership today.

It is time to return to the original meaning of the word power if we want to create a workplace where humans are able to be in order to do necessary and meaningful work. And it is time to modernize the practice of leadership if we want to be able to create the environment to support those efforts.

When the world health crisis first hit in March 2020, I found myself, like many others, on a great number of Zoom calls. As a drama researcher who studies human behavior and whether or not the behavior of humans adds to business results and group well-being or diminishes results and/or workplace happiness, I found myself in a fascinating position. I was able to observe informal interactions happening in the first five minutes of every call while waiting for all invited to show up and for others to figure out their microphones and video feeds without the participants being inhibited by having an observer present. It was a rare seat in the house to observe the interactions between participants as people gathered, forgetting that they were visible to me.

In the beginning, I was touched as I watched a majority of the people join, reach out, and connect in really cool ways, asking each other how they were doing, if they had all they needed, providing encouragement, and even offering large gestures of assistance at times. Colleagues were kind, caring, looking for ways to serve one another, even coaching each other in the use of the new online platforms. For many of us, the universe had put us in a big "Time Out," and we were making great use of it to refocus on what was important in life, to get intentional and focus on making sure we as people were cared for and then finding new ways to connect and incredible ways to innovate. The theme in the air was "together we can, and no person left behind," and it was quite encouraging. The energy was peaceful, the people confident and centered, the language positive, and the actions seemed intentional.

In spite of all the pain that came for many from the pandemic, I was seeing some highly conscious leadership behaviors. Perhaps there were some blessings that would come out of the great falling apart of 2020—the un-precented times seemed to have people in touch with their own values and clear about serving others. Many were taking time for their own development, doing a better job setting priorities, and accepting their external limitations but refusing to be defeated.

And evidently, this was not easily sustainable.

About five months into the pandemic, now coupled with social protests, the darkness of winter, and big truths about racism and social inequities in our country and workplaces, the first minutes of the meetings had completely changed in tone. The focus was no longer checking in to ensure all were okay and then figuring out creative ways to succeed in spite of the circumstances. And the informal chatter often extended long after all were accounted for and most were Zoom fluent.

People took turns bemoaning the state of the world and the state of their own lives. They talked of being bored or being at the mercy of their kids and partners. Many colluded, complaining about the lack of leadership in national efforts and in their own organizations. Others pined to go back to a world of "normalcy" just like it used to be in spite of all of the flaws of the old way having been exposed. The conversation was usually a lot of agreement that someone should do something and that the best strategy was to hope for the best. The only tips being given out were recommendations on best Netflix series. The rare times ownership showed up on the call is when someone confessed to "going over the wall" to get together with friends and travel to better destinations.

The core theme had become: "Ain't it awful. These times are so hard. Someone should do something." It was such a change in tone and energy and, quite frankly, results. This wasn't just a bad day or week—I was on 4–5 different calls in different organizations each day, and I found the trend very concerning. The effect of the incredible circumstantial disruption of the early WFH days had worn off, and most were adopting strategies of just making it through until somehow things got better. People were impatient with one another, setting harsh boundaries at times, while others were disengaged, claiming Zoom fatigue while cutting people down in private chat entries.

And so, I revamped my message and stepped up each time I heard this dark cloud start to set in, "Hey everyone, great to see your sweet smiling faces. We have important work to do here so let's begin with good choices. Cameras on, private chats minimal, no lurkers, everyone participating in the chat room, and polling providing updates. Let's start with everyone typing in two feelings they are feeling and why if you are comfortable. I realize I am not your formal leader, just a guest invited to help with morale. But now that I have your attention and participation, let me set the tone and make the invitation.

"Yes, these are tough times, *but these are our times*. We are here right now, complete with all of our intersections of all that we are with the experience and brilliance we bring for a reason, on purpose. The chapter being written right now is our chapter. How this all plays out has to do with us and our choices. First, we have to own that these are our times. And then we need to focus on what great would look like. What if we could build a better workplace and world place together? What has this pandemic revealed to us about ourselves? Who has been reflecting on where they need to grow next and got busy with that development? Let's manage our energy away from why we can't and why we shouldn't have to and let's invest it in how we could—let's dream a bit about how we could.

"What most people don't understand is that way more often than not, people emerge from traumatic situations grown and transformed for the better rather than stressed. It is called Post-Traumatic Growth (PTG), and leaders have a huge role to play in this phenomenon. To fuel PTG, we need to help **hope** make a comeback. As a leader, we deal in hope, in the belief that people are amazing and have great potential and we set about helping them grow and emerge impacted but not traumatized. Resilience is being developed in the challenge with support, coaching, and reflection.

"I want to help hope make a comeback and am confident that together we are collective genius—who's in?"

I did this many times a day—with a lot of kindness and an open heart—and the energy of the meeting changed. At first people got quieter, then they got peaceful. They quietly contemplated and realized they had fallen off their path, and then they stepped up and focused and created some really great things together. It isn't that I am some great leader or fantastic motivational speaker; it is that I have learned the techniques, practices, and strategies to see and accept reality for what it is—at times, unpreferred. I have learned to resist the urge to argue with that reality, thereby wasting a ton of energy and opportunity, and to focus on co-creating great results by calling people up to greatness. But to do this day in and day out takes a disciplined set of habits and dedication to stay ready as a leader.

Traditional leadership philosophies won't work in the new world. Leadership is sacred work, and those who are given the privilege and positional power over people's work lives need to be seekers who are willing to cultivate higher levels of consciousness in themselves and others.

Leaders have two main roles to play in this brave new world: They need to "love people up" and they need to "call people up." And to do that well and consistently, we all need to live as seekers, involved in our own evolution.

We need a sustainable way to lead from a centered, peaceful place regardless of our circumstances. We can't rely on disaster to manufacture ideal behaviors. *Becoming a Peaceful Powered Leader* is a masterpiece in teaching you how to do just that. It is time for all of us to move away from traditional leadership philosophy that tells insecure leaders what to do and say and that allows unenlightened people to have the title of leader. It is time to modernize leadership philosophy to ensure that those who lead are doing the internal work of evolving—emerging with hard-won wisdom—and can step into the mess, own it as theirs, and bring out the best in the people on their teams to succeed in spite of the circumstances. I absolutely love this book. Jared does a phenomenal job laying out the path to personal evolution and points the way to calling your people up to greatness.

This book is an incredible tool that will help you modernize your leadership philosophy. A modern leader realizes that one can never really manage people, so they strive to manage the energy of people. Instead of only focusing on how they want to impact the world, they allow themselves to be evolved by the world. A modern leader is one who has done the self-reflection and the internal contemplation necessary to make sense of their world, along with the inner work to forge it all into wisdom. A leader who uses this wisdom gained from inspired seeking beyond their own ego so they can walk freely into the imperfect, messy world with a lot of love.

Leaders believe in and build capacity in others. They teach them to stop bemoaning unpreferred realities and wishing for different futures and show them the sometimes very small space in which they can embody empowerment, find agency, and contribute to a better world place and workplace regardless of circumstances. Sure, they help change the reality when possible but, more importantly, they teach people how to walk through the world more skillfully. For that is the ultimate freedom—to be able to generate internal wisdom and peacefully occupy an external position of love and to be skillful enough to walk through the world regardless of its current state.

The space where wisdom lovingly meets the world is a peaceful space—we need more of it, and we need more leaders who can help create it. Do your own work and then help others do theirs. We need to emerge from all that we have created and experienced evolved, not traumatized.

I have high regard for Jared's work; this book is a significant contribution to leading others in a kind and sustainable way. And I have high regard for Jared Narlock personally. The world is a better place with Jared in it. I know firsthand that he practices what he preaches, shows up as human and aspiring, and is a Peaceful Powered Leader. His experience and this book are a wonderful contribution to the conversation we all should be having on modernizing leadership as a philosophy and as a practice.

Enjoy the book and resist the urge to immediately envision who in your life will benefit—spend the time and do the reflection. You will come to understand that changing yourself will change the world around you in really significant ways. Your true power is in cultivating the ability to be—master that and any suffering will end.

Cy Wakeman
President and Founder of Reality-Based Leadership and *New York Times* bestselling author

Introduction

P ayday! This day has significant meaning to any working person. While most want to love their jobs, they also want to get paid for doing them. Payday is a highly anticipated and important event whether it is weekly, biweekly, or monthly. People expect to be paid, and in many cases, they *need* to be paid, consistently and on the day promised.

While payday has a straightforward meaning for most, for me, it will forever represent a step in my path to growth as a leader. On an early spring morning, a payday morning for the organization I was with at the time, I found out what type of leader I really was.

I held an executive leadership title, and I thought of myself as a pretty good leader. I had a highly engaged team, we delivered the results asked of us by our Chief Executive Officer (CEO), and we had a favorable reputation in the organization. I must've been doing something right—right? That morning, though, I found out the difference between being a good leader when things are going well and actually being a Peaceful Powered Leader.

At the time, I shared responsibility with another executive for leading a joint division for the organization. In partnership with our finance team, our division had been working for almost a year to implement a new enterprise resource planning solution (ERP). This term—enterprise resource planning solution—is a fancy way of saying a new software platform that allowed our finance, human resources, and supply chain systems to easily interact with each other, making both our lives and our customers' easier.

That spring day was the first payday after the official launch of the ERP system and the first time we used it for distributing payroll. I woke in the morning excited to see my paycheck deposited into my checking account. As I hit the numbers on my mobile phone to log in to my account, I had a feeling deep in my stomach that the money wouldn't be there, but my blazing optimism quickly pushed that aside.

I was in my banking app scrolling down my various accounts to my checking account and . . . it wasn't there. I hadn't been paid. I quickly texted one of the two executive leads directly in charge of the ERP project to let them know. They thanked me for the heads-up.

While I wasn't an official project lead, I was, along with another executive, clearly tied to the project. In that moment, I said to myself, "I'm glad I'm not a project lead! People didn't get paid and someone's going to face heavy interrogation on why." This defense mechanism and thought process are not responses I'm proud to share. In that moment, I wanted to distance myself from the ERP project as much as possible. I knew our CEO was not going to be happy about this snafu. The essential part of the new ERP launch was to ensure the first payday went smoothly, because people needed that paycheck and they deserved it.

While deep down, I knew I was an owner in this process, I kept telling myself, "It's not my problem. I don't have to face our CEO with answers. Those other two will have to do that." My morning went on as I continued to get ready for work.

Upon arriving at work, I headed to the office of one of the two project leads and asked if there was any news. The lead said it wasn't clear what had happened, but they had been told the payment would come into people's accounts and there was no need to worry. This was around 8:00 a.m.

By 8:15, I had a line of people outside my office—my team—asking why they didn't get paid and what was going on. I quickly told them I had been assured the pay would be deposited soon. Nine o'clock came, and no payment in people's accounts. At 9:15, I started to see the nervousness in the project leads' faces and could hear it in their voices. At 9:30, our offices were inundated with calls from employees asking why they hadn't been paid. Some couldn't get into work for their shift because they had no gas in their car and no money to put gas in it.

At 9:45, I found out our CEO was communicating with the two project leads and he wasn't happy. He also wanted to know why no communication had gone out to employees about the situation. One of the project leads stated there was no need to worry; the payments were coming, and communication wasn't needed. As 10:00 approached and calls continued to flood the division phone lines, my team asked me to act.

One of my team members came to me and said, "Jared, this isn't okay. We have to communicate to people what is going on. We have to help people who are in need right now. People are stressed that their automatic payments aren't covered because they weren't paid this morning. Please communicate something so they know they aren't being ignored and we are working on this."

I sat there. Just a few short hours ago, I had been sure of how great of a leader I was, and now I sat in fear. In my head, I started to blame the two project leads for not taking action and communicating what was going on. I blamed them for not running a test to ensure the system worked properly and people were paid accordingly (they actually had run a test, I found out later). I sat thinking, "I'm going nowhere near this disaster because I don't want my name on it or the backlash that will probably come from our CEO." I sat there thinking of myself and only myself. I was nervous, I was afraid, and I was anything but peaceful. I wasn't leading in that moment; I was cowardly sitting behind my desk waiting for something positive to happen.

I finally got up and talked with one of the two project leads and said we needed to get the other project lead on the phone and make something happen soon. I did this but also did everything I could to make sure my name wasn't attached and I had no fault in the situation. It was now past 11:00 and approaching lunch hour for team members, and still no communication had gone out. Our public relations team asked if they could help with sending out an update, but unfortunately, nothing was prepared.

I acted boldly on the conference call. I absolved myself of any wrongdoing and made sure the project leads knew this was their fault and they needed to own it and do something quickly. I was assured everyone would get paid that same day. I stayed humble on the call but with full internal ego, trying to explain to them how some banks would only pre-deposit the money on that day. A deposit is not immediately available until the next business day at my bank, and many others would have that same problem; this wasn't okay.

I had two of my star team members on the call, and I was trying to make sure they knew how much I cared about our employees. The truth was that I cared for others greatly, but in that moment, what I cared about most was ensuring I didn't get blamed. I was choosing service to self, through self-preservation, over serving others.

Communication finally went out to the organization, and people were promised in writing that they would be paid that day. However, there wasn't a timeframe for when. I'll never forget a courageous team member coming into my office and asking me to do something for the people who needed help right then and there. The team member asked whether we could buy gift cards to give out in case we weren't paid on that day.

As tears rolled down the team member's face, they shared with me a memory from ten years prior of being a single parent and waking up with no food for their young child and no money to purchase food. I could see the team member replaying that experience in their head and could hear the pain coming through their voice. I asked what they expected me to do and calmly this team member said, "Lead."

It used to be so hard for me to relive that moment. I couldn't share it openly. I was ashamed of my actions, and for a long time, I was still the same person I was on that payday. Maybe I grew in some ways, but I couldn't confidently say that if I were put back in the same situation, I would handle it differently.

I wasn't a different leader. I wasn't a person leading with peace. I was a person leading with fear. Fear of losing my job for doing the right thing when the right thing exposed my mistakes. I was a leader who felt confident as long as I could keep control. I took care of my team the right way most of the time, and I had the engagement scores that supported that feeling, but in that moment, as that team member stood in front of me, I knew engagement scores meant nothing. I had the team's trust, and in one critical instant, I lost a great deal of it. I also lost a lot of my self-trust. I talked a big game, but that was just my big ego talking.

I was a scared leader, who hid behind the knowledge I had, the previous accomplishments I'd gained, and the strategy I'd developed to ensure I was successful without ever really having to step out of my comfort zone. I was a leadership wimp, not a leadership warrior, and being a U.S. Air Force veteran, it was hard to look at myself in that moment. I was carrying a lot of shame.

Employees did get paid around 2:30 p.m. that day. The incident came and went. From my understanding, the whole snafu came down to one box, one little box without a checkmark, causing the whole process to fall off course. This never happened again while I was employed there; nevertheless, the whole situation caused a lot of mistrust amongst our employees. The CEO did talk with me and the other executives attached to the process. He understandably wasn't happy and made sure measures were put in place to keep it from happening again. He also made sure there were measures in place to properly communicate in a timely manner with employees if something similar ever did happen.

I didn't take the brunt of the criticism because I had accomplished my goal. I had ensured my name was not associated with the snafu by not leading in the moment. Although in one way, I felt comfortable—*at least I'm safe*—I wasn't the person I once thought I was, and I wasn't happy about that. I also wasn't sure how to fix it.

I left my role as an executive soon after. At the time, I thought I knew why. I knew I wasn't at peace, and I thought it was because I was far removed from my purpose to help others grow and develop so that I could inspire them to take action in the areas of their lives they wanted to. I even shared this in my book, *People Powered Moments*, as the reason for walking away. I was always an accountable person; however, I made sure to stay in my safety zone as much as possible and that made it much easier to be accountable.

After the payday incident, I spent the next two years in search of peace. I longed for an inner peace that would allow me to be the kind of leader and person who the team member who stood in front of me with tears slowly moving down their cheeks could be proud of. I wanted this for this team member and for the many others I coached, led, and served, including my friends and family. What I learned, though, is that I needed to do it for myself. I needed to have a mirror moment and stop placing my happiness and the peace associated with it into someone else's hands.

This book is a culmination of the research I came across, the learnings I discovered, and the actions I took to reach a place of inner peace. It focuses on what has allowed me to transition from a motivational poster of knowing the right things to say to truly becoming a partnering, gritty, courageous leader who connects the how and when to what. Finding peace is not an easy process. It involves a lot of wrestling and discomfort but is ultimately rewarding and freeing. This book is an active learning exercise designed to help people on their journey to finding their own peace.

While this book doesn't offer a step-by-step guide to peace because each person's path is different, it does offer a way for you to step out of comfort, not into discomfort, but instead into courage and change, if you choose to. There are actionable strategies to support you during each step you take on your path to inner peace and becoming a Peaceful

Powered Leader. But to get to true comfort, brave and gritty comfort as I like to call it, you have to first take action.

Taking action usually involves failure on the way to success. If you're not ready for real failure, which often comes with judgment, criticism, and ultimately, learning, close this book now. Its words will have little meaning to you if you aren't ready. However, if you are looking for change and are ready to act in courage, proceed forward and get ready for some wicked hard self-discovery; know I'll be here with so many others celebrating you!

We may not know each other yet, but we've heard about each other. We are the people who others share stories about. We are the leaders who are often nameless but have had impact on others' lives through truly leading for others and putting service to others above self-preservation and service to self. We are the Peaceful Powered Leaders, and I invite you to join us. It is always your choice whether you step in or stay outside and hope and wait. I hope you take that step. If you do, buckle up and get ready to ride courageously to your inner peace!

I want to be very deliberate in calling you a learner right now. I don't want you to just read this book. I want you to apply its teachings, your learnings. My purpose in life is still to help others grow and develop and inspire them to take *action*! Taking action was, and is, the key to opening up the doors that changed me and my life, and that included the journey to inner peace. I still struggle at times with inner battles that threaten to rip through the peace I've found; however, three key components have helped me stay active in living a life powered by peace, not validation. They are:

- Discipline
- Time
- Action

I had to have the discipline to change aspects of my life that didn't promote the peace I was looking for and the peace I now know. I had to apply discipline to inspect my thoughts and the stories I tell myself about my relationships, including the relationship I have with my career. Discipline has been at the forefront of the healthy boundaries I've created in my life, like not judging others for their boundaries, decisions, or choices. There's much more to developing this discipline that we'll explore in the components involved in becoming a Peaceful Powered Leader.

Leading with discipline helped me to create time where I once thought there wasn't enough. It enabled me to carve out time differently in a life led by peace. Time is mine to own while I have breath and well-functioning motor skills. This is a reality that so few have decided to step into and own. We hear stories of leaders who have done it, and if you are like me, you've often thought they were lucky or fortunate in the hand life dealt them, until you hear the statistical data that refutes that claim and pushes us toward accountability. They weren't lucky—they were disciplined.

As I've created time, I've found learning is much easier. Not in how I learn but in ensuring I have set aside time to keep doing it, to keep growing and investing in myself and others. With time, I've opened the door to self-reflection, which allowed me to challenge myself and look for why I was living an unsettled but prosperous life.

Discipline and time have led me to a place initially filled with terror. Once I found that I had discipline and time to do what I was seeking to do, I realized I could take action. I had to put the work in. In the past I took action for validation; now I was seeking to take action for self-growth and to find the peace I was longing for. Finding out how to let go of control and let in peace was now within clear sight. The journey hasn't been easy, hasn't been done alone, and has left me without some of the people who used to be in my life.

This book is a journey. It requires you to be active throughout its pages. It is a guide to help you become a Peaceful Powered Leader for yourself and those you have the privilege to lead. It is not a judgment on where you are right now. Others can judge you, but it's what you choose to hold yourself to that matters. Before you continue to read, stop and ask yourself the following three questions. If you can't say yes to each one, consider why you couldn't say yes and decide if you can get to yes.

1. As I read this book, am I able to make it an active process?

Are you ready to take notes? Are you ready to answer the associated questions? This is not a passive read. You can read it passively, but it probably won't get you to the place you hoped to reach when you picked up this book and paid the retail price for it. You saw something of worth in the title or back cover; you bought it for a reason.

Grow your investment by deciding how you are going to make this an active reading process. You'll be learning from my experience and research as a certified coach and leader in multiple arenas. Additionally, you'll have the value of learning from thought leaders who I've had the opportunity to connect with in my journey. In some chapters of the book, you will find a thought leader interview, where some of the most amazing speakers, authors, and organizational leaders provide their insights and learnings to help illuminate the topics at hand. You are in for a treat, as these are some inspiring human beings!

2. How are you going to discipline yourself to finish this book in one month?

This book isn't meant to be read in one sitting. It is also not meant to be read partway through in two weeks and then picked up again in seven months. Not that anyone else does this, but I know in my earlier years, I would often find a good book, start it, find myself at the bookstore two weeks later, and bring home two new books to start the cycle over again. You can read other books while you are reading this one, but I recommend reading it in a month's time, working through the action steps toward discipline, time, and action.

3. Are you giving yourself permission to have fun?

Remember when I said my journey often involved learnings from others? Well, this question is a learning from one of those individuals.

One of my favorite teachers is author and researcher Dr. Brené Brown. I had the opportunity to learn from Dr. Brown and her research and learning materials. It was an exhilarating two and a half days. I learned from her how important it is to be vulnerable and to be honest with ourselves and others. I also learned from her the importance of giving ourselves permission slips to have fun.

This journey will cause you to do a lot of self-reflection. It will cause you to push yourself to places you maybe haven't been before. What you will find may be pretty heavy for you. Growth comes with discomfort, but discomfort can also be fun. This is your journey. Feel free to be silly at times. You'll need moments to have a laugh. In my experience, these will be when you look back and have a good chuckle about your journey.

As you prepare yourself to begin active learning in self-leadership and leadership of others, get ready to challenge some norms. I'll share some of my initial insights and invite you to dive deeper into these by completing exercises in self-examination throughout the book. Don't worry, I will guide you through the exercises (and expose some of my own weaknesses along the way). We are partners in this learning journey.

What Makes a Peaceful Powered Leader?

I've got an "easy button" for that! Remember the ad campaign about using the easy button? That ad tapped into the fact that getting stuff done can be difficult and it would be awesome if we could simply press a button and make that work easy. The company that promoted this campaign did a great job of bringing the philosophy into their stores. In their ad campaigns, they also did a wonderful job of showing what the opposite of easy looked like. In my experience, portrayals of leadership are often similar to those ads.

Most of us are great at describing real-life, sincere, and specific examples of what poor leadership looks like. However, when I ask people to come up with examples of great leadership, I often hear textbook answers that sound like a checklist. Why is this? Is it because so few of us have actually experienced excellent leadership? Maybe we just haven't stopped to think about it because we've been consumed by the power of poor leadership and are struggling to escape that reality.

The answer may vary from person to person, but right now I am going to ask you to let go of what you know, or who you know, that comes to mind when you think of poor leadership and start embracing becoming a Peaceful Powered Leader. In this book, I'm going to give you the shell of a Peaceful Powered Leader. You will have to put in the work in each section to, piece by piece, fill in the shell on your path to fully embracing Peaceful Powered Leadership. Just as I've had to do the work to get there, and still work day in and day out to grow there, you've got to do the same. Continuous learning is a section of the shell that you must find out how to fill and connect with. We are going to start with awareness of what makes up the shell of a Peaceful Powered Leader, so we can dive into each distinct piece.

1. Peaceful Powered Leaders set and own their reality.

Those who want to know peace in their lives must be willing to set the course of action that will take them there and realize they own that action. Accountability is the foundation of Peaceful Powered Leadership. This means being accountable for your thoughts, actions, and the steps you choose to take. Individuals moving toward peace stay away from storytelling in their lives and work to manage their ego. They step into, and live in, reality and the facts associated with that reality, not assumptions, opinions, or made-up stories. They learn to separate the fiction that feeds egos from the facts that, when embraced, can help lead to actions and solutions. These people understand their future is in their hands, for them to set. If they have a goal, they know they have the opportunity to reach that goal.

Peaceful Powered Leaders have confidence in their skill sets because they regularly focus on developing them. They don't rest on old successes but instead work to grow, with an understanding of how that growth can help those they lead and themselves step into greater opportunities. These leaders are far from perfect, but they are active and work to stay on the path of owning their story and their reality, knowing it takes work and a continuous effort. Peaceful Powered Leaders don't compare themselves to others or put people down. Instead, they understand their growth is in their own hands. They stay on the path, recognizing that they can control their destiny, and walk forward with a mindset of ownership.

2. Peaceful Powered Leaders build others up.

These leaders don't stand in comparison or competition with others. Instead, they stand in the awareness of a reality where they have the power to help, influence, partner, and ultimately build others up. These individuals find joy in the ability to reward others, and they stay on the lookout for ways to bring forth sincerity and consistency in the process. They do not see others as competitors, but instead as opportunities for connection, with rich possibilities. They pick up the phone to call a stranger who they heard was influenced by their work and tell them they are rooting for them. These leaders have had success on the path to their dream and seek, knowing full well there is nothing in it for them, to help someone get past a barrier on the path to their dreams. It's the leader who checks in on her employees day in and out, doing what she can to give them the courage and inspiration to bring their best forward, while also surprising them by sending a handwritten note to their home with words of thanks and encouragement. It's leaders who also step into partnership with others to move beyond giving words of encouragement to helping with actions whenever possible.

3. Peaceful Powered Leaders put service to others ahead of service to self.

One of my favorite books comes from one of my favorite leaders, Simon Sinek. In his book, *Leaders Eat Last*, he captures the essence of putting others first. Sinek examines the thought process of leaders who understand that a large part of their role, in fact, the very foundation of it, is serving others. Many call this concept, explored by Sinek, servant leadership. I like to think of it a little differently and use the term *service leadership.*

From my experience, service leadership is easy to talk about but one of the toughest to enact. Leaders can say they are in their role to take care of others but are untested until faced with a decision that creates the fork in the road, to either do what's right or what's easy and safe. I've been there, and as I shared in the opening story of my payday experience, I failed in that moment. I didn't serve others but instead chose myself. I wasn't at peace then. I know the decision would be much different today. Putting service to others ahead of service to self may seem like a sacrifice at times, but if we are holding true to our values, it shouldn't ever seem like a compromise.

4. Peaceful Powered Leaders invest in others.

This piece of becoming a Peaceful Powered Leader is where word meets action to build and extend trust. Building others up is important, and many leaders I've worked with have admitted it is much easier to do than truly investing in others. Investment takes time.

It is vital to reward and recognize those we have the opportunity to lead. I was at a conference a few years ago, listening to an executive from a well-known hotel chain share the following: "I've been asked by leaders what is the right amount of reward and recognition to give others. My response is more. More is the right amount, regardless of where it is currently." I agree, and I also have found that some leaders are great at reward and recognition but struggle to invest their time in helping those they lead develop and grow.

In my work over the years with teams, it's become evident that employees love recognition, but they want to be invested in too. According to Gallup, one of the leading experts in employee engagement research, 59 percent of the current generation coming into the workforce rate opportunities to learn and grow as extremely important to them when applying for a job.[1] They want to know that their leader wants to help them grow to a point that they could lead the team or walk into the next role, perhaps on another team. The Peaceful Powered Leader holds development time with others as sacred time and is even willing to sacrifice "face time" with a prestigious name if it conflicts with time scheduled in service to and investment in those they lead.

5. Peaceful Powered Leaders set sacred time with themselves.

Investment in others is vital and highly valued by today's workforce. While Peaceful Powered Leaders understand this, they also understand they must invest in themselves to continue to grow and evolve, not only for those they have the privilege to serve but also for themselves. It's hard to help others grow if we ourselves aren't growing and developing. This is accomplished by establishing sacred time. Peaceful Powered Leaders have worked to develop a level of discipline in setting aside time and establishing patterns that allow for continuous progress. Time that isn't easily given away or pushed to the curb. Time that is focused and filled with deliberate actions toward building routines and patterns. These patterns include reflection on what went well in recent events and what may need adjustments moving forward. Time to establish processes for strategy building to help best lead their teams and support their organizations. They don't fly by the seat of their pants, going from one meeting to the next, but instead prepare during sacred time toward thoughtful and strategic approaches. They establish patterns that allow time for personal development, to expand their thought leadership through reading, writing, connecting with others in their network, and much more. They develop routines to ensure their families, their communities, and other areas of their lives aren't sacrificed to their careers. There is no work–life balance for them because it is all life to them.

I've never embraced the term work–life balance and have found the majority of Peaceful Powered Leaders don't either. Drawing a line between our work and life is an unhealthy thought pattern. It essentially challenges us to think that work is the one component that is separate from every other aspect of our lives, instead of realizing work is a big portion. Peaceful Powered Leaders understand this and have brought the same grace, understanding, and ability to withhold judgment into their workplace relationships that their team members would expect to experience in other relationships in their lives.

These leaders understand and model this behavior. They don't watch a clock to ensure their employees are meeting the minimum number of hours expected. Instead, they partner with them to help ensure needed outcomes are met. They help get the work done and also model that it's not at the expense of the other areas of their life. They model this through establishing healthy boundaries around their sacred time like leaving the office early to go see their child's drama production or to pick them up on the last day of school to celebrate another year of learning and accomplishment. They know they can leave the office because they have a team that will continue to move things forward, just as they encourage those they lead to practice the same healthy habits that ensure well-being. They don't look for more time in the day because they've put the effort in to make their time count as needed and have it become more and more meaningful through establishing a sacred time process.

6. Peaceful Powered Leaders empower themselves and create an environment for others to succeed.

These leaders don't make excuses; they build on what they have established as Peaceful Powered Leaders to create options. They model empowerment by creating plans, trying things that may or may not work, learning from their failures, and keeping their focus on what's in their scope. They continue to find a way. So often we are confused in our understanding of what empowerment truly is. It is not getting to do things the way we want to do them, without scoping or accountability. Because so many of us have this false view, we believe, and say, that we are not empowered. Empowerment, though, is finding a way. Peaceful Powered Leaders not only find a way for themselves, but they also find ways to help those they lead understand they have the power to create, build, and own solutions instead of excuses. They help people grow into a mindset of optimism and the belief that what is ahead is within their control to reach and accomplish. This may sound like a tough thing to instill in someone, but actually, it is not so difficult when you have already built those people up and invested in their growth and development.

Becoming a Peaceful Powered Leader is not easy. It involves a lot of failing, a lot of screwing up, persistence in resisting your ego, allowing yourself to have some fun, and commitment to active development work, all fueled by courage and candor. This book is designed to provide key strategies to help you get to peace through your own work. Reading the book will do absolutely nothing for you, beyond providing awareness that may lead to self-reflection. The action, though, the work to get there, is on you. You have to own it and make the choice to take action on the plans laid out.

There is no magic pill, and it doesn't happen overnight, but if you truly dedicate the time, effort, and energy to a disciplined process and are willing to step into vulnerability, you can have peace. And as I said before, I'm here for you each step of the journey.

A key point to remember, and something I learned from my research, is that all six steps to becoming a Peaceful Powered Leader work together and the most vital is step one: Peaceful Powered Leaders set and own their reality. Every other element is built on this foundation and made possible by it. I found that the people who lived this were able to successfully take the next steps.

Conversely, I found in my research that those who didn't set and own their reality did not consistently achieve the next steps. They struggled to build others up because they were unsure of themselves and didn't believe that they owned their outcomes. Many of them were fearful someone else might outshine them, so they fell into only lifting up those they didn't view as competition.

They were very self-serving, looking over their shoulder, choosing self-preservation over service to others. They invested in others sporadically. When someone asked for help, if they had the time and didn't view the person as a threat, they would help. More often, though, they were too busy to help and too busy even to invest in themselves. This often led to storytelling and providing nonfactual reasons about why someone received a reward, recognition, or promotion instead of them. They viewed events as happening to them, as opposed to happening with their input or even as a result of their leadership. This thought process hindered their ability to step into empowerment and own what they were doing. It was a full-circle process with the root of their problems being they didn't think they could own or set their reality—or they weren't willing to try.

I share this because this first step, presented in the first chapter you are about to read, is so vital. Give it the time, attention, and effort needed. It is the game changer. It will require time for you to digest and reflect and work. If you only have ten more minutes to read right now, don't go any further. Schedule some time. Again, you got this!

Now, let's go do it!

Chapter 1
Peaceful Powered Leaders Set and Own Their Reality

Have you ever thought about what your ideal situation would look like? Without realizing it, many people do on a regular basis and share their perfect scenario with others. You can tell when you are having an ideal life described to you because it is often accompanied by phrases like "Once I achieve this, then . . ." or "I just need this one thing, then . . ." and I am sure you can think of a few others.

As a leader, you may have heard something similar from your employees when discussing the increasingly popular topic of employee engagement. You ask your employee what would make them more engaged, and they say, "If this one thing happens, then I'll be more engaged." Sure, until that thing happens and they decide they need one more thing. The key phrase in the previous sentence is "they decide." The power of choice to be engaged is in their hands. No one can make them engaged; they have to choose to be. We can influence with the environment we set up for them, but it is still their choice. This is true for leaders setting and owning their reality as well. They have to decide.

Are you an owner in your career? Do you really challenge yourself and your thinking about this? I want to share an experience from about a decade ago. I was discussing the topic of ownership with a group of employees in an organization. I asked who in the group were owners of their jobs. As usual, when I asked this question, most hands went up. I then asked if anyone in the group had ever owned their own business and had employees whom they paid. One hand cautiously went up, and I started to dialogue with this individual.

She shared that she had a business selling a particular line of products to customers and she, at the company's peak, had eleven employees working in her business. I went on to ask her what she did at the company she currently worked for. She shared that she was a customer service representative. I asked what that meant, and she explained that it was her responsibility to work with customers to get them help if they needed certain product information and assist them in any way she could. I then shifted the conversation back to her business.

"How important was each customer interaction when you owned your business?" I asked.

She responded, without hesitating, "Extremely important. I went to bed some evenings not knowing if I was going to be able to make payroll for the eleven employees working for my company." She went on, "Every interaction, phone call, email, and in person interaction was so vital. Every cent mattered." As she shared, I could hear the passion in her voice as she was reliving this experience.

I then asked this individual if she treated every interaction, phone call, email, and in person interaction with the same level of importance in her current role. I could see her reflecting for just a quick second and start smiling a bit nervously. "You got me" she said. "I raised my hand when you asked if I own my current role, but I don't. I don't treat it like I did when I owned my company."

"Why is that?" I asked her.

"Because I haven't chosen to. There is no difference. Every cent, every interaction, still should matter the same." I was proud of her for saying this, as it took courage in that moment. She knew my intent wasn't to make her feel bad but to help the room see what a real owner looked like. In that moment, she owned that she wasn't owning her role the way she could be. She said, "I am going to change my thought process around the way I approach my job going forward."

Just like that woman, people allow themselves to live in the story that they aren't in control of their reality. They believe their work is set by their leader or their goals are chosen by their organization. The true owners though, choose to be fully accountable to themselves in all areas of their life, including their careers. They know they can set the path for their work and the direction they and their team will take. This takes real ownership.

Think about it. As the owner of a company, do you wait for direction to be given and then come up with your strategy, or do you build strategy and set the direction to go in? If you are still in business, I am going to bet you chose the second option from that previous sentence. Why then do leaders not follow this same approach in their careers?

As a leader, you can own your role. You can put the time, effort, and energy in to set the direction for your team. You can go to your leader and show them the path you are taking with a well-laid-out strategic plan you've put on paper for them to see. You can provide them the next steps, instead of waiting for them to provide those steps for you. So many, though, fail to make this choice and live in the reality of letting others set the direction for them. They tell themselves stories like, "You don't understand, my boss would never let me do that." My question to them is, "Have you ever asked or tried that approach with your leader?" The response is the same almost every time: No.

These individuals are telling themselves stories about why they *can't*, instead of putting the work in to own their reality and figure out how they *can*. Those who take their reality back into their own hands, both in thought and action, are able to live with inner peace. They know they are in control of next steps, and they also have committed to accepting ownership when those steps may not go the way they wanted or expected.

Let's examine ways that you can work toward fully owning your life. This is the foundation for actual peace. I want you to examine and reflect on whether you are stepping into or out of ownership in some key areas. As you consider these aspects of ownership, work to keep the perspective that this process is about *you*. It isn't about someone else. Own that right now. Also, approach ownership with a focus on what you are doing. It's not about what you *aren't* doing; it's about what you *are* doing and if what you are doing isn't aligned with what you want to be happening, *you* have the power to change that. What you do impacts the outcomes of what you get in your life. Let's look at three qualities of owners in detail.

1. Owners grow.

One of the toughest comments to listen to is: "That person is a born leader!" That statement couldn't be further from the facts when we look at people who are ownership leaders in their lives. Instead, I prefer Vince Lombardi's quote, "Leaders are made, they are not born. They are made by hard effort, which is the price which all of us must pay to achieve any goal that is worthwhile." People who choose to be owners know that they have to continue to grow and evolve. That includes knowing when to ask for help when something is beyond their current capacity. Owners spend time and energy working toward growing new skills, improving upon current skills, finding ways to gain new knowledge, and understanding that this all takes time. Goals aren't achieved overnight, and growth isn't either.

Owners don't play the victim when they don't get what they want. They embrace failure and look for the next step to get closer to their desired goal. I apply for numerous speaking opportunities every year. I get a good number of them and also get rejected by an even larger number. I could easily blame the groups who reject me and say they aren't forward-thinking or they always book the same people. The reality, though, is I don't know why they made their choice. I usually try to find out why and sometimes people will share, which helps me reflect and grow. Other times I don't get a response. I don't give up because I have a goal, and I still have a lot of growth options to pursue on my way to that goal. That is how I own the situation. I can decide to give up, or I can press forward. How I act, respond, and move toward next steps are all my choices to make, and as I continue to press forward, I look for ways to grow.

I want you to take a few moments and reflect on what I like to call "My Trying Resume." We so often associate growth with our career, but those who set and own their reality understand that growth comes in all areas of our lives, and it isn't always through success. It also comes with failure. At the center of both is how we tried.

People often forget how many tries it took to learn from failure or reach success. Think about a big goal you accomplished. An owner recognizes that their plans, when grounded in reality, aren't usually going to go in a straight line from A to Z. They know there will be bumps, bruises, celebrations, ups, downs, smiles, and tears. Peaceful Powered Leaders acknowledge these pieces may be a part of the journey, and that's okay. They embrace them all.

2. Owners pay attention to what they say.

While not every word that comes out of our mouths will be the perfect one or the wisest, we still have the opportunity to be mindful of what we say. Owners are deliberate in word choice. Take a moment and think about someone you admire who seems to accomplish a great deal of what they set out to. Think about the words they use when they are describing their goals or ideas. I would venture to say that the majority of people who come to mind use action-oriented words. We are in charge of our story and what we choose to put out into the world through our words.

How do you keep forward movement toward your goals and ideas? People who struggle in ownership tend to use words or phrases like "I can't do that and here's why" or "If only this would happen." These words don't elicit ownership. When we use them, we are leaning on reasons why we can't or constructing a false reality where the right circumstances must fall into place.

Owners, on the other hand, use words that help them push toward the next step. They use phrases like "I am doing" or "I choose to." When a bump or barrier gets in their way, they don't bail; they question and seek solutions. They ask, "What did I learn from that experience?" or "What's another way I can approach this situation?" or "How can I take the next needed step in this situation?"

Peaceful Powered Leaders are deliberate in their words because they understand the power of words, both as an owner in setting their reality and as an example to others. Are there words or phrases you are currently using that make it hard for you to stay in the mindset of ownership? How can you replace those words with ownership?

3. Owners understand choice.

Choice is something we are faced with every day. Some leaders have worked to limit the number of choices before them each day by creating routines—what they wear or eat—to ensure they aren't spending valuable time they could use making more consequential choices. No matter what routines we put in place, though, we are still faced with choice after choice.

We have a choice whether to be accountable to others. We have a choice in how we speak to ourselves. We have a choice in how we speak about others. We have a choice about how much time we dedicate to a particular question or answer. We have a choice in how we embrace each feeling or emotion that presents itself to us. Knowing this reality, many people choose to walk through life as though they don't own the power of their next choice. This is not the case with owners.

Owners step into and stay in a reality in which they understand that the choices they make are theirs. This is a key component of becoming a Peaceful Powered Leader. These leaders understand that they own their fate. They plan accordingly to be ready for what may come at them next and work to be proactive so the next choice is made *by them* instead of *presented to them*.

Owners also understand they have choice in how they embrace their feelings and emotions. I used to believe in the mindset of always being positive. I started to learn, though, that peace was not only owning how I feel but also owning how I embrace those feelings and trying to do so in a healthy way. Nataly Kogan, author of *Happier Now: How to Stop Chasing Perfection and Embrace Everyday Moments (Even the Difficult Ones)*, explains that research shows becoming happier in life is something we can own, and by embracing three principles, we can choose to grow in happiness. The principles Nataly shares are:

- Happiness and emotional well-being are not extras—they are the foundation for being your best self and doing your best work while navigating life's ups and downs.
- To truly thrive, you need to stop trying to turn negatives into positives and learn to embrace the full range of human emotions.
- Happiness is a skill, not just a feeling, and you can strengthen that skill with practice![2]

In order to set and own our reality, it is important to understand how to own our emotions. Too often, we try to step away from emotions we think are negative, like sadness or frustration. However, it is through embracing these uncomfortable emotions that we understand them better and process them in healthier ways. As owners, we accept that in order to do this we must make the choice to practice and work toward growth with all emotions. This allows us to embrace an uncomfortable emotion and still be at peace about the situation we are going through. Strength comes from embracing the emotion and handling it in an appropriate and respectful way, not pushing it down and telling ourselves to stay positive. Positivity doesn't necessarily lead to peace.

I remember one day sharing a new process with a group of leaders. As I was explaining the process, one leader rolled his eyes and sighed over and over again, until he eventually said, "This process is a joke." I was a little taken aback at first, because it didn't feel like he was being respectful. I worked to remain curious instead of judgmental, though. I asked him what he meant by this statement, and he proceeded to share that the process wouldn't work for his team because of the number of people he oversaw and we (meaning organizational development and human resources) didn't understand how his team was different.

He didn't provide any concrete facts or data on why the process wouldn't work. He only gave generalities that appeared to involve his opinion on the matter. I asked the rest of the group if they were feeling the same way and they shared they weren't. With that response, I let him know I'd welcome discussing his concerns further after the meeting, out of respect for everyone's time.

After the meeting finished and he and I were one on one, he proceeded to tell me that "the process sucked." I had a choice then—a choice to own the reality in front of me and confront it or to let him continue down this path of behavior and remarks that didn't seem to be backed by facts or data. Remember, Peaceful Powered Leaders set and own their reality, and part of that involves owning our choices.

I shared with this leader that I'd like to discuss his concerns, but before we did, I wanted to address my observations. I shared that I noticed him rolling his eyes and sighing multiple times in the meeting, and I asked him why this was. I was seeking to understand. He told me it was because he was frustrated. I then asked him if he kept saying the process sucked because he was frustrated. He said, "Yes." This next piece is very important in owning our reality and influencing others' reality.

I shared with this leader that I'm always open to feedback and it's okay if he doesn't like or agree with something I'm bringing forward. What is not okay, though, is bringing these behaviors and poor word choices forward. He stared intently at me for a moment. I then shared that I would like to hear his feedback and I would like him to remember that we both wear the same badge and are in the same company and on the same organizational team together. (We weren't in the same department, and a theme that comes up sometimes in organizations is an "us versus them" mentality. I always try to remind people we are all ultimately working together toward the same goal and remove the "us versus them" mindset.)

I told him I was there to help him. I explained that the process was backed by data and research, and at the root of it, the process must start from a regulatory standpoint no matter what. I added that I wanted to make sure he felt comfortable and set up for success with it. He continued to stare intently at me. He appeared to be contemplating something. And then it happened.

He proceeded to tell me he was nervous about failing. He said his scope was really big as a leader, and he was afraid of what would happen to him if he didn't get the outcomes the new process required.

I had a feeling this may have been the underlying issue. It often involves fear when someone lashes out negatively about something that will impact them. There is a difference between someone being critical with facts and data and someone lashing out with opinion. Be sure to pay attention to this as leaders.

He was lashing out because he was afraid. He was wrestling with owning his reality in this process, and instead of owning it by asking for help, he was owning it by lashing out. Earlier in my career, I would have pushed back in the meeting and avoided him after. I probably would've gone back to my team and talked negatively about him. That process doesn't lead to peace, though. Seeking to understand, assuming positive intent, and choosing courage and candor over arrogance and anger will almost always set up your reality for better outcomes. I'll discuss these points further later on, but for now, I just want to focus on the role power of choice plays in the story.

Earlier in my career, I could not have responded to this leader the way I did. I had to expand my toolbox of skills, grow my mindset, experiment with new approaches, and work on how I set and owned my reality. I still didn't handle the situation perfectly, and I learned from it, but I was able to connect with the leader and we worked on a solution together.

That leader was known for putting processes down and lashing out with negativity toward new things, even prior to our interaction. As we finished our conversation, I told him the following: "I am here for you. In the future, if you start to struggle with how you will reach what is expected, that is okay. Don't push back at the person delivering the message. Instead, come share with me why you are struggling, and we can work together to get a solid plan in place." The leader sincerely thanked me.

Sometimes he did come to me, and sometimes he lashed out. He didn't change overnight, but because I addressed the situation, I now had the opportunity to own my reality and help him own his each time he struggled. I share this example of growth because it took a long time for me to achieve it. It wasn't easy. In fact, the path of storytelling and using emotion over data and putting others down because they offered criticism was a much easier path for me, as well as my colleague. It wasn't peaceful, though. It wasn't leading either, and I had to own that and change it. You can too, and there are active strategies in this book to get you started.

Again, this book won't solve all problems, but it will provide a foundation for evaluating why you may be out of peace and how you can step back into it. The key takeaway in this section is to set and own your reality. Take your time with this step. If you don't work to hardwire it, please don't expect the other steps to have as great of an impact. However, just like I told the leader who felt overwhelmed, I am here to help you succeed. So, let's start working on it together by going through the first exercise.

Taking a Deeper Look Exercise

Challenge yourself to own your reality as you move through the exercise below. It asks you about your typical responses to situations.

Your ego may creep in as you answer, and that's okay. When it does, push back. Remind yourself this is for your growth and there is no development without honesty. Also, there is no rating at the end of the exercise. It's not about a score. Each of the ten questions offers two approaches, and you circle the one that most often represents your view. Take time to write down why you feel this is the case. Try to think of specific examples of when you held that perspective or gave that response. What habits are in place that make it easier for you to adopt one outlook as opposed to the other?

Questions:

1. Circumstances happen to me. – I create the circumstances I step into.
2. I live more by the motto "What happens will happen." – I live more by the motto "What would it take to make this happen, because I'm going to do it."
3. The phrase "Why is this happening to me?" comes out of my mouth regularly – The phrase "How can I own and impact this situation?" comes out of my mouth regularly.
4. I think "What is the worst that could happen?" – I think "What is the best that could happen, and how can I make it happen?"
5. My mind leans toward "How can I serve myself in this situation?" – My mind leans toward "How may I serve others in this situation?"
6. I focus on the end result of needed outcomes in business. – I focus on how the process can help me learn and grow and how I can have fun with it.
7. I don't take time regularly to reflect on what's working well and what I'd like to work on changing. – I regularly take time to reflect on what's working well and what I'd like to work on changing.

8. I allow parts of my reality to be filled in by stories that I don't fully have facts to substantiate. – My reality is based on facts that I know for sure.
9. I look for answers to problems as quickly as possible. – I ask myself questions to ponder and explore potential root causes to problems as I try to solve them.
10. I don't tend to think people are regularly trying to give their best. – I believe people are generally always trying to do their best and their best may look different from one day to the next.

Take some time to reflect on your answers. You may have circled one choice while thinking, "I don't *always* do that, but I do it more than the other choice." That's okay. Reflect on what you like or don't like about the responses you chose. Are you happy with them? Do you want to make changes based on your reflection? Now, here is the big question: Are you currently owning and setting your reality? If you are not, what can you do about that? Be sure to capture in writing your thought process as you are asking yourself these questions. You may want to refer back to your notes as you venture through some of the other exercises.

Owning All Outcomes

Once leaders take this first step of setting and owning their reality, they must next prepare themselves to own all outcomes. Peaceful Powered Leaders know that with the choice of ownership comes the choice of trying and trying brings with it both failures and successes. As owners, we must own both the good and bad outcomes.

Remember my payday story? If I had owned that situation and tried to seek solutions and communicate to employees as I should have, there still would have been a very real possibility that people weren't going to get paid that day. If that were the case, I would have had to face that outcome and my CEO's reaction to it. But if I really owned my role, I would have had to act. I couldn't have just sat quietly while employees wondered what was going on with their pay.

Regardless of the possible outcome, Peaceful Powered Leaders choose to own rather than make excuses. They've learned how to move past storytelling and blaming others. They look to learn from failures and acknowledge the facts of the situation. This process doesn't just happen overnight. It takes deliberate action and effort. I still find myself sometimes saying out loud, "Okay, Jared, let's stop right here. I'm not really owning this right now." I utter those words because I've learned over time that helps me stop and reflect on what true ownership in the moment looks like and allows me to adjust as needed. Many times, I don't want to adjust, because I can see that the next decision I'll face will be a hard one. It may cause discomfort, it may upset someone, and it has some unknowns, like the ultimate outcome. However, choosing to truly own the situation also feels good, because I am connecting to my values and I am able to stay in peace knowing I am being accountable and serving others first.

Another part of setting and owning your reality as a Peaceful Powered Leader is not working to control others. Peaceful Powered Leaders are confident in themselves. I once worked as a consultant with a leader who, unfortunately, in each individual and group interaction I had with him, would put someone down. I was asked by his supervisor to work with him and other leadership team members that reported to her. After a few interactions with the team, I sat down to discuss next steps with the supervisor and go over themes I had seen. I explained to her that I would be happy to coach all individuals on her team, except this leader. I went on to explain that all were open to development and the partnership approach I take around letting go of unproductive approaches, except this individual.

In my interactions with him, I watched him try to control and dictate every step a member of his team took in meetings. I watched him try to control the flow of the leadership team he was a part of and at times put others down in a passive-aggressive manner when they were recognized by peers for doing something well. I provided specific examples to ensure there were facts to reflect on and work from.

The supervisor admitted she had seen this too, but felt the leader was so smart he could work through the problem. I told her I agreed he was smart, but he did not have the confidence needed to step into growth. This leader felt his only path forward was one of control over others in all situations.

This person appeared to have an internal battle raging within. He was wrestling with doubt, asking, "Am I good enough?" To combat the doubt, to feel good enough, he tried to dominate every situation. Needless to say, this is not setting and owning reality. He appeared to be afraid that others would find out he didn't know something or had more to learn. Putting others down or working to control each movement of his direct reports was his comfort place, and he kept his direct reports from development opportunities through his actions. This type of wrestling is a far cry from peace.

A Peaceful Powered Leader is someone who owns their peace and understands that while they can influence others, they can't control them or the decisions they make; they can only control their own reality. They can't control what others think or say about them, but they can model how they want to be treated. Let me be clear on what influence means here. Have you ever watched someone try to "win over" a person who has criticized them or their work? It is a tiresome process, and I can speak from experience. I have watched many a high performer receive an abundance of positive feedback about a project or presentation, only to watch them turn around and feverishly try to win over the one person who said they didn't care for it or it didn't resonate with them. The best response to feedback, even feedback perceived as negative, is "Thank you."

Let's explore a story together from a blog post I wrote a while back. It is titled "Stop Trying to Win People Over: 3 Steps to Own Your Outcomes." It is a story about Janice. Janice was asked six months ago to lead a project for her division. The project had a large impact and implications for her organization. She did a great job collaborating with those willing to partner. She also tried to communicate with and bring in those who showed little interest in the project. In the end, the outcome and results of the project were a huge success.

Many in executive leadership praised Janice for her work and what it was doing to help the organization. Additionally, multiple other leaders at different levels of the organization congratulated Janice and thanked her for what she was contributing to the company. Even with all this praise, a small number of leaders criticized Janice's work.

Guess who those people were? They were the same people who had showed little interest in the project. They had chosen to not engage in the communication methods Janice used. They chose not to provide feedback at different steps in the project when Janice provided opportunities. Now though, as Janice achieved success and the project's results were moving forward, their criticism was rising. That criticism was from less than 5 percent.

With an abundance of feedback on what went well and comments from the 5 percent who didn't feel the same, what do you think Janice decided to focus on? You guessed it—the feedback coming from the 5 percent who didn't even engage in the project. Why do so many of us follow Janice's path? Why, instead, don't we listen to the criticism, be respectful of it, give it the room in our thoughts it deserves (in this instance, 5 percent), and move forward? Janice should have been celebrating, but instead she tried to win over her few critics. My feedback to Janice is "Stop!" And here are three reasons why.

1. The 5 percent had the same opportunities as the other 95 percent.

So often, we try to win over the critics, but if you pay attention to the truly successful in leadership, sports, business, or whatever area you choose, they build on their success by continuing to grow with those who believe in them. They listen to the critics to find nuggets that point to ways to improve, but they don't try to "win them over" because they understand they've had the same opportunity as those who are supportive. That 5 percent who didn't want to engage or participate in the opportunities presented to them are the same people who complain that the free cheese and pepperoni pizzas brought in for them aren't bacon and pineapple. Stop trying to please those few and keep focused on working with the people who want to be accountable, respond to the opportunities in front of them, and engage.

2. Work with those who want to engage.

If someone doesn't want to partake, let them sit on the sidelines. Ensure they understand the consequences of sitting on the sidelines and move forward. Those who want to engage have decided to step into ownership and help you achieve the goals and desired outcomes. They want to be there with you. Embrace them, partner with them, and celebrate the failures on the way to the successes. Remember, failure and success aren't at opposite ends of the spectrum; they both are part of the first step of trying, and if we keep trying, we will succeed in reaching the needed outcomes.

3. Learn to appreciate when you've done something that elicits feedback.

Sometimes we believe we fail because of the feedback we receive, but we forget that receiving feedback means we did something to elicit it, which is more than most can say. Embrace the critics too and celebrate that you got a reaction, whether you characterize it as positive or negative. You know where you wanted to be and what you wanted to accomplish. If you got the outcome you were aiming for, own it, celebrate it, and be accountable for it, even if it wasn't what some thought was needed.

While these three steps are easy to write about or talk about, the reality is that it is hard to hear criticism, especially when our ego tells us it isn't warranted. Embrace the feedback and remember that you stepped into ownership as a leader. Peaceful Powered Leaders use feedback to grow and are at peace with their performance in the moment. If it wasn't their best, they acknowledge it and what they will adjust in the future, but they don't put themselves down. They realize it was their best for today, and that is okay. They own their reality and move forward, because, again, they understand both success and failure lie in trying. They did the thing! So often people try to win others over and it keeps them from stepping into peace.

At the end of some chapters, I've included an interview from a thought leader who has clearly demonstrated how they work toward and own the topic discussed. These sections will be labeled "Thought Leader Perspective." I've had the opportunity to learn directly from some of these individuals, and others I've learned from their writings, workshops, or seminars. Each brings a unique perspective, and from my interactions with them and their works, I can tell they care about serving others and helping others grow. I'm thankful for the opportunity each of them provided me to interview them and include that material in this book. Each interview adds another learning perspective to becoming a Peaceful Powered Leader, and I encourage you to expand on your growth by connecting further with these individuals and their work. Let's jump into the first of these interviews.

Thought Leader Perspective – Cy Wakeman

Cy Wakeman is president and founder of Reality-Based Leadership and a New York Times *bestselling author. You can learn more at LinkedIn: Cy Wakeman; IG: @cywakeman.*

Narlock: What's your view on the ownership of reality and how it impacts people's lives?

Wakeman: In the moment, if you step down and see yourself as a victim of that reality, then it doesn't even dawn on you that it's your responsibility to serve others, or lift them up, or empower them. It's like your only temptation is to collude with them about how we are victims and then wait for someone else to come in and lead people through this. Whether you step down or up in that moment determines whether you see it as your responsibility to do these other things like serve and empower.

Narlock: How do you see the thought process differing for leaders who own their reality versus those that don't?

Wakeman: I talk about low self and high self and how people toggle up or toggle down. When you are seeing the world through the lens of your ego, it's hard to consistently muster up and do these things—like serve, uplift, empower—as if they are automatic behaviors. However, when you are toggled up and seeing the world through your real level of consciousness, you're using all of your intelligence, and these behaviors are almost your natural state. It's really your natural state once the drama is gone.

Like most leaders, if you're not viewing through the lens of ego, your natural state is to do these things because your heart is wide open and your mind is wide open. You see someone struggling, you don't go kick them if you're in high self, you go help them. A lot of things that I'm teaching become effortless if people are in high self. But how do you get from low self to high self? Through self-reflection, and self-reflection is what drives accountability.

Owning your own reality and releasing your circumstances aren't the reasons you can't succeed; they are the reasons you must succeed. Stop arguing with reality and instead toggle up to self-reflection and you will start to own your accountability. It increases in stages. As you take each of these steps, owning reality becomes more effortless and you live more in your natural state.

Narlock: Why do you think some people are scared to step into the accountability and own that?

Wakeman: They don't know how their mind works, so they don't know how they are being played by their ego. They are believing everything they think, and their ego is giving them very corrupted information. If you were seeing their reality the way they were, you would see that it was scary, but most people don't realize they're not the thinker. They're the ones serving the thinking. So they are watching an illusion and they think it's real. They are going off of corrupted data. They are making reasonable decisions based off of corrupted data.

Once they understand how their mind works—that their ego is always playing them and running these corrupted takes—once they quit believing everything they think, and they learn to question their thinking, then it breaks the hold the ego has. It loosens the grip the ego has on their world, and they start to see so many other possibilities, and then it's not as scary. For instance, if you're watching a horror film and you're a little seven-year-old kid, you're not going to walk outside at nighttime because you think that fantasy is real. How can we be entertained by a horror film as adults? Because we know it is fictional. But if you're a little kid living in that horror film and the illusion is so powerful that you get scared and you actually scream out in a movie theater, your mind has forgotten that it's not real. Or if you are watching a magic trick, once you understand how the illusion works, it is hard to go back and believe in its reality again.

People don't understand how their mind works, and we don't understand how the world works. Most people don't jump into accountability because they don't understand how their mind works. They think they can argue with reality, but reality will win 100 percent of the time. Once leaders understand how their mind works, and how the world works, they can move through the acts of leadership much more skillfully. I think that people believe the feelings come from believing reality. You're believing what reality is, but your feelings are coming from your story, not the actual thing that happened.

The first responsibility of a leader is that they really need to become better users and consumers of their own mind.

Narlock: What's the difference in thought between the business owner and a leader in an organization?

Wakeman: People have gotten the definition of empowerment wrong. People think that empowerment is their leaders giving them power to do something, but that's an old philosophy where you need to wait until someone empowers you. My definition of empowerment is stepping into the power you already have. And the ego looks for why we can't. And leaders need to look for how we can. So when a person is in ego, the whole energy is why they can't. The old philosophy for leaders is that we manage people, but we actually manage the energy of people. And we need to manage our energy and other people's energy away from why we can't to how we can.

Again, it really all starts when you are toggled down; you are seeing the world through the lens of ego. You are in low self; you are using the most primitive form of your intelligence. And you don't see a lot of places you can plug and play. You just see, because you can't change everything, that you can't change anything. It's the way the ego really keeps us safe because the ego sees the world as made up of villains and victims and sees us as victims.

When you are in high self, you can see all this opportunity. All of these things that you could plug and play and have impact. You could get out of learned helplessness and get into having impact because you are seeing the world from a high level of consciousness, which starts with self-reflection. Self-reflection is the foundation of accountability; it starts with that. When you are accountable, you are usually asking very different questions like "How could I?" and "What if it was possible?" and "What if I did own my own company?"

The way you get that person from "I can't do this" to "How I could" is you get them into self-reflection. What if this was your company and you owned it today? What would you do then? Why aren't you doing that now? We never get the perfect results, but when we start taking away our excuses, we are learning, and learning will play into our future results. When we stay in excuses, though, those excuses legitimize us playing small. And when the excuses aren't there because they aren't real—they are just creations of the ego—then we are unlimited in our potential, and we have no reason to play small.

Chapter 2
Peaceful Powered Leaders Build Others Up

Putting others down is a singular activity, while lifting others up takes partnership to move words into action. Peaceful Powered Leaders step into partnership and make the choice to lift others up. The joy in their journey comes from service to others, not service to self. One of the first downtrodden moments in my life was witnessing a former leader of mine take credit for something they didn't do.

I had left a team, but not the organization I worked for, because a really cool, new opportunity had come my way. Although I had moved on, I still highly respected my former team leader. In my new role, I participated in a meeting where my former leader presented some awesome material that I knew was put together by one of my old team members. When the meeting finished, an executive asked the leader if they had produced the work. The executive wasn't focusing so much on the content as the look, feel, and flow of the documents. In that moment, I heard my former leader confidently say, "Yes, I have been working on my skills in this area and I put together every piece you saw!" The executive showered them with praise.

I was taken aback. Why would this leader lie about who put the material together? The leader had a great opportunity to lift up one of their team members who had this awesome skill set. They had the chance to let them shine. Additionally, as their leader, they could take joy in knowing they had a piece in helping the team member get there. Unfortunately, this was not the route the leader took, and as the months went on and my blinders fell away, I started to see many characteristics of a leader far from inner peace and struggling with ego management. This leader seemed to be looking for any chance to self-promote in an effort to get promoted. Think about that for a moment.

If, as leaders, we are spending a large portion of our energy self-promoting, then what do we have left for building up those we lead? What I've seen in my research of great leaders who appear to have embodied Peaceful Powered Leadership is that they don't need to self-promote for two reasons: (1) their focus is on service to others, not self, and they have clear connection to that purpose and (2) they don't need to self-promote because those they lead do the promotion for them.

Leaders who lift others up have strong ego management, and they have teams that value them and praise them both in words and actions. These teams deliver amazing results and tend to receive recognition, which includes recognition of their leader. Whether the leader likes praise or not, it naturally comes through the process of serving others. Although this praise may not always be as direct and public as the praise self-promoters receive, it does come. Regardless of where, when, or how the praise is delivered, Peaceful Powered Leaders carry with them the practice of ego management.

Our ego loves to tell us that the world revolves around us, and so many people give in to the ego. I know I have done so often over the years, and I still do at times. Peaceful Powered Leaders, though, regularly work on their development and understand that, as discussed in Chapter 1, living in peace takes ownership and accountability. There are four key development strategies that you can step into right now to start managing your ego and ensure you are focusing on those you lead instead of yourself.

1. Commit to your own success and define what it looks like for you.

So many leaders struggle with comparison. When we have difficulty defining what a goal looks like for us, we often substitute what it looked like for someone else instead. When we do that, we don't have a clear purpose or understanding of why we want to achieve the goal, and we open the door for comparison—and the ego loves comparison.

Comparison, with the ego's help, will tell us someone else achieved a goal because of an opportunity given to them that we didn't have or they didn't deserve. Comparison will take us down a path of inventing why that person was able to achieve the goal. In contrast, managing our ego focuses us on ourselves and how to own *our* reality and reach *our* success. Comparison often leads to putting others down while ego management keeps us building others up. Comparison will also keep us from working toward our dreams.

I admire many people in the fields of leadership development, organizational psychology, and social sciences. When I was starting out, I would often compare where I was in my journey to where I thought they were. I say "where I thought they were" because there is absolutely no way we can know where someone else is. We don't know the journey they have been on, the work they have done, and so on. Recognizing we don't have a full understanding should easily keep us from comparison, but, unfortunately, as you and I both know, it doesn't. I would regularly compare myself with the people I looked up to and think, "I'm not good enough to be on the stage they are on or coach in the type of organizations they coach in." What I found, though, when I stepped out of comparison and worked toward defining what my success looked like, was that I was on the right path for me. Something else pretty awesome happened too. Many of those people I admired built me up—each in different ways. One called me unexpectedly on the telephone to simply offer words of encouragement for the work I was doing and to let me know they saw me. Another chose me to be a part of their street team, providing me the opportunity to grow through their investment in me while I helped others learn their wonderful teachings.

One actually wrote the foreword of this very book! Another became my coach and eventual mentor. I realized through all this that the people I was comparing myself to weren't my rivals but were Peaceful Powered Leaders who were building others up!

When we practice ego management, competition with others diminishes. We can define what greatness looks like for us and hold our purpose close in pursuit of goal achievement. We are also able to celebrate if someone else gets to that goal before us because we understand *their* journey is not *our* journey.

2. Keep your narratives in check.

Those who practice ego management are great at sticking to facts and have developed the ability to challenge their stories through practice and growth. I don't know about you, but I have a pretty creative mind when it comes to storytelling, especially when the story involves me. Growing up, I would take a boring event and add detail after detail to it in order to make it more exciting. This was a car trip game I played in my head as I looked out the window from the backseat of my parents' car driving back and forth on Interstate 75 from Valdosta, Georgia, to Tampa, Florida, to visit my aunt on long weekends.

While this process helped me pass the time of the almost four-hour trip, it didn't serve me well as I got older. I started to take pretty straightforward situations and let my storytelling ability, now powered strongly by my ego, run wild. This wild run often led to me villainizing someone who I felt was keeping me from getting where I wanted to be. I would stress over situations, and, at times, I would put others down in an effort to feed my ego.

The peace, though, that came with keeping my narratives in check was amazing. I found that as I started to challenge the details of my story and pull out the true facts to move forward, I had a lot more energy. I wasn't stressing over things and felt so much better about how I could own my reality in situations. Because those situations were rooted in truth, they were easy to manage, and my focus stayed on what was important. Through this process, I realized I could use my extra energy to help others. My narrative was no longer revolving around me and was easy to sift through without the false details I had been introducing.

3. Commit to working toward healthy ways of embracing emotions.

Emotions come in all shapes and sizes, and it is important to embrace them all, but in appropriate ways. As we work to strengthen our ego management, we have to release old habits in pursuit of building new ones. If we allow our narrative to be dominated by jealousy, for example, when something awesome happens to someone else, we have to work on a way to shift to a new feeling of excitement for that person.

Let me be crystal clear here: We can still be sad the opportunity didn't happen for us. Many today are pushing the need to be happy all the time and shift our "negative" emotions. Studies show, however, that the process of embracing a wide range of emotions can be better for our health. It is important to acknowledge emotions like sadness when we feel them. The challenge, though, is to keep our narrative in check while acknowledging our emotions.

It is so easy to let our ego run wild and tell ourselves a story that the other person wasn't as good as us and shouldn't have received an awesome opportunity. That is not a healthy process. A healthy process would be to acknowledge that we are sad because we wanted this opportunity. But we didn't get it, and that is okay. We still own our reality and next steps. We can celebrate the person who did get it because that is their reality. And that's it. No storytelling about why they got it or why we didn't. No comparison of their abilities to ours. This process allows us to genuinely lift others up while still taking care of ourselves.[3]

4. Find out what additional strategies work for you.

While I just shared three core strategies for practicing strong ego management, each person is different. I can tell you that if you practice the three strategies over time, with a real development mindset, and are being honest with yourself through the growth process, you will see improvement in your ego management. But you may need to add strategies specific to your strengths and weaknesses.

For me, early on in the process, I found I had to share with vital friends the false narratives that were going on in my head. I struggled to decipher what was real and what wasn't because I had become so skilled at storytelling from my car trip game. Some of my vital friends would help me challenge my stories until, over time, I was able to start doing this on my own. It was hard the first time I decided to share my false narrative with someone else, but I wanted to be a better leader for others and knew ego management was a key piece to reaching that goal. I couldn't consistently and genuinely lift others up if I was worried about their success outshining mine.

Ego management isn't easy to develop. The power of storytelling is all around us—on the television, in the movies, on the internet—and we often handle situations the way we were taught by these false narratives. However, we can work on its development just like any other skill if we choose to pursue owning our reality.

The Power of Gratitude

Another component of Peaceful Powered Leadership closely linked to building others up is gratitude. Here's a quote I often hear repeated, both because of how powerful it is and how amazing the person who said it was: "I've learned that people will forget what you said, people will forget what you did, but people will never forget how you made them feel." The wonderful leader and poet Maya Angelou spoke these insightful words, and I have found them to be so true. Sometimes it is a grand gesture and sometimes it is a short conversation, but however and whenever wholehearted gratitude is given, it has the power to fuel others and leave a lasting impression on people's feelings.

The great leaders work to stay in the mindset of service to others through the power of gratitude. Gratitude takes practice, but it plays a large role in shaping your outlook and your inner peace. Research done by Dr. Rick Hanson, professor of psychology at the University of California, found that building a practice of gratitude results in the following benefits:

- Contentment becomes stronger than dissatisfaction.
- Peace becomes stronger than frustration.
- Appreciation becomes stronger than criticism and complaining.
- Resilience to life's challenges increases.[4]

I would say those are some pretty awesome outcomes. Even with research showing these findings, people struggle to bring gratitude into their daily lives. Let's take a moment and go through a gratitude exercise before delving further into the topic.

Reliving Gratitude Exercise

This exercise has several steps and they all involve writing, so it's time to find a pen and some paper. As you work through the steps, please accomplish each one before moving to the next. I will do the exercise along with you to provide an example. You will see my own response below the directions for each step.

1. Think of a time you were genuinely grateful for something someone did for you. Pick a specific event or action. Write down the experience, capturing details of what happened.

My experience – My friend Andrew gave me the gift of running a Tough Mudder obstacle course race with me. I had just moved to Oregon and away from Andrew and the rest of my obstacle course team in South Dakota. After I moved, I signed up to do a Tough Mudder in Seattle. What most drew me to Tough Mudder racing was that while the structure of the races encouraged you to challenge yourself, it wasn't about you beating out other people. It was about you helping others. I really didn't want to run the race alone, but I did want to experience its beautiful location. I asked Andrew if he would be interested in joining me in Seattle to run the race. I knew he and his wonderful wife, also an obstacle course racer, were expecting a second child in the coming months, so I wasn't sure joining me would be an option for him.

We communicated back and forth. I could tell he wanted to come, and I so badly wanted him to. I knew running this event with him would create a joyful memory. He and I had been workout partners in South Dakota. There had been days I didn't want to be in the gym, and then I looked over at Andrew. He always seemed to be thankful for the opportunity to be there. It didn't matter if we were doing an uneventful piece, like running for two miles as part of a larger workout or smacking a sledgehammer against a tire, Andrew was always present in the moment. I admired this about him; he appreciated the experience. I knew he would be the perfect race partner. Andrew came to Seattle, and we had a blast running the race.

2. Reflect on why this experience was important to you and write down your thoughts about it. You may have done some of this already in section one, like I did, and that is okay.

My experience: Andrew knew the move to Oregon had been hard for me and was there when I needed a friend. I am so grateful for him and the time we spent together on that beautifully muddy course. Our days together in Seattle greatly deepened our friendship as we shared about family and future goals and had many laughs. He took true interest in what I said. He saw me in that moment and showed up fully present each and every step we took on that course and during the weekend together.

There was one point during the race when we were running through a forest and it was raining. It wasn't a hard rain and was actually quite calming. I, however, wasn't thinking too much about it as I was running, when all of a sudden Andrew said, "Hey, let's stop and take this in." I wasn't sure what he meant at first, but I stopped. He turned to me with a huge smile on his face and quietly said, "Look around. How amazing is this right now. We are in Seattle together, in the woods, rain coming down gently. Everything is so green. This looks like something out of the movies." I started to take it all in. He was exactly right! It was such a beautiful sight. It was a sight I probably would have missed had I been on my own. Thankfully, I was with a person I had learned a lot from about being fully present in the moment. This moment, and the entire experience, is something I am so grateful for.

3. How did you feel about the person when the experience occurred? Try to relive some of those feelings and describe them in detail in your written response.

My experience: I was astonished by Andrew. I remember being so excited when he told me that he was going to come to Seattle to run the race with me. I was smiling from ear to ear sharing the news with my wife. I called her right away to tell her because she knew how badly I wanted a partner to run the Tough Mudder, and it was really going to happen. I remember the excitement of seeing Andrew approach my vehicle at the airport when I picked him up. It was a place of comfort.

As Andrew and I ran the race, we smiled almost the whole time. I remember so much of the day with vivid fondness. There is an obstacle on the course called "Artic Enema." It is literally water with ice in it, or ice-cold water. I remember when Andrew and the rest of our team went through the obstacle together at the first Tough Mudder we ran, miles outside of Las Vegas. The impact of hitting the water, being submerged from head to toe, takes your breath away. Your body has trouble processing what is going on because it is so cold. I didn't want to do the obstacle in Seattle. Andrew knew me well, though, and he knew I would regret not trying. He calmly looked at me as we approached it and said, "I'll pass by this with you if you want to, but I have watched you overcome obstacle after obstacle in life in the years I've known you and this little one right here is nothing for either of us. We are here, so why not do it?" He knew exactly how to motivate my heart.

It wasn't peer pressure; it was caring. We jumped in and the feeling I remembered the first time came rushing back. We were done in seconds, though, and I was so thankful my friend helped me remember the confidence I had and that he was right there with me.

4. How did you show your gratitude to this person? Write down your response.

My experience: I thanked Andrew over and over. I tried to pay for as much as I could during our time in Seattle. He kept telling me that wasn't needed and he was so happy to be there with me. Anyone that knows me, though, knows that my love language is gifts. I'm not always great about expressing feelings in words, so I try to do it in action. If someone has received a gift from me, it was thought out and has meaning and purpose. I love to gift experiences to people over tangible items, but, ultimately, I just want them to know how thankful I am. I wanted Andrew to know how much I appreciated him, his company, and his care.

5. Now write down how you felt reliving the experience. You know the drill. Be specific and use descriptors.

My experience: Writing this particular memory down brought me back to that moment, and I realized I was smiling again ear to ear as I put pen to paper. Recounting the race, I felt admiration for Andrew's grit and determination. I was ecstatic remembering how we rocked on that obstacle course. I felt the confidence he inspired in me, which allowed me to run races on my own after that. Sometimes as I'm struggling to meet an obstacle on my own, I return to our moments running that race together and find I am not alone in spirit. I didn't know that race with Andrew was going to give me confidence far beyond what I ever imagined. I've since run three obstacle course races alone, three half marathons alone, and two full marathons alone. These were all things I wouldn't have done without Andrew. By lifting me up through that entire experience, he helped me find new confidence and perspective about working past my limiting beliefs. I feel forever grateful. Thank you, Andrew!

So, what is the point of this exercise? Its purpose is to help shift your mind to peace. Practicing gratitude takes work, and we are going to explore it further because Peaceful Powered Leaders aren't perfect. They do, however, have life practices that keep them in peace or able to return to peace very quickly rather than to frustration. It's hard to be frustrated when you feel grateful. Each time I have gone through this very simple exercise with people, even when they are frustrated, it brings them to a sense of peace in the moment. It allows them to center differently and think through the events that led to frustration in a different way. I still encourage them to embrace the emotions they are experiencing because that is a healthy process, but we are working to embrace our emotions with accountability, facts, and objectivity. When we focus on gratitude, it does a number on our ego and makes it hard to become frustrated. Gratitude often allows us to more easily embrace the harder emotions in healthy ways so we can move back to the emotions we like to embrace.

Grateful Leaders

Gratitude actually plays a significant part in the way we lead because it affects both our physical well-being and the way we model our leadership for those we serve. According to research by psychologist Robert Emmons from the University of California-Davis, something as simple as keeping a gratitude journal and writing regularly in it about moments of thankfulness can significantly increase well-being and life satisfaction.[5] With a tool as powerful as this, why aren't people embracing the practice more frequently? Simply put, gratitude is something that must become a habit in order for you to feel the benefits on a consistent basis. It takes practice and growth, and like many pieces of growth, people fail to put the time, energy, and dedication into making it a habit. Let's explore why it's one of the most vital pieces of stepping into and staying in the mindset of Peaceful Powered Leadership and how you can make a habit of gratitude.

Gratitude affects the brain in positive ways.

According to research conducted by the National Institute of Health (NIH), feelings of gratitude directly activate brain regions associated with the neurotransmitter dopamine. You may have heard that dopamine makes us feel good, but what I learned through NIH's research in my journey to becoming a Peaceful Powered Leader is that dopamine is also important because it pushes us to move to action.[6] When we exercise gratitude, we essentially get a shot of dopamine, which increases the desire to do the thing we just did again. We are teaching ourselves that it is good to show gratitude, and we are teaching our brain to focus on potentially spreading kindness. We are creating a cycle that pushes us to seek out opportunities to be grateful and spread kindness versus looking for things to be ungrateful about.

Gratitude helps keep us centered.

Have you ever felt mad or angry while being grateful? It is really hard to do. Why is this? Let's stop and think for a moment. What if, when you were mad at someone, you took a step back and thought about how grateful you were for them. I'll share an experience I've had with this practice.

One day, I was extremely frustrated with a friend. Her communication style wasn't connecting with mine over the last few weeks, and I moved out of accountability for my feelings and into blame for her actions. I didn't like the way I was feeling and knew my emotions were centered around my ego and the stories I was telling myself about this person, but I couldn't shake it. I kept telling myself this person was being unkind, lacking in thoughtfulness, and didn't care about me. Finally, I challenged myself to move from frustration back to peace. I sat down and wrote out experiences with this person that I was grateful for, because she had truly done so many amazing things for me over the years.

By the time I finished writing out my grateful experience, I was wearing a big smile. I called the friend and shared with her how thankful I was for her. I then did share that I had been telling myself a story around our relationship and it had put me in an angry place. I was able to tell her this without frustration or animosity. I shared how I owned my story and moved from anger to gratitude. She was thankful I shared, and we were able to continue our conversation and feel a wonderful connection.

Gratitude is an opportunity to serve others in a different way.

Gratitude can help us and others. I've researched and have been a part of conversations about whether gratitude was really self-serving or service to others. I believe it is both. We've already explored that gratitude can have a huge impact on our lives and the way we feel. It also can have those same impacts on the lives of others. As leaders, it is vital to express gratitude to those you serve. I live by the belief that we never know fully what is going on in someone else's life and that people are always trying to do their best. Their best may look different from one day to the next because of what they are encountering.

When I was an instructor in the air force, I remember a student of mine who made a lasting impression. He was twenty-seven and just made the cutoff to be in the U. S. Air Force at the time, if memory serves me right. He was one of the hardest workers I had ever met. He wasted no time in the classroom. If it was study time, he was studying, while so many others used the time for social interactions. He was often the last person to finish the class exercises because it was clearly hard for him to grasp the material we were learning. One day, I watched as time was counting down on the progress check he had to complete to move to the next section. After each person finished, they were excused to the break room while others completed the checks.

With fifteen minutes left, he was the only one left in the room. Then there were ten minutes left. Finally, with just over two minutes left, he completed the progress check. He passed with the bare minimum passing score. He was relieved. I had had faith that he would pass, and I had a small thank-you card waiting for him when he did. In the card, I wrote that I appreciated his work ethic and that while these courses were hard, his approach to learning, study habits, and overall attitude would get him through. I wanted him to know whether I was his instructor and class leader or someone else on my team was, I was there to help in any way I could. I believed in him because I could tell he was owning his learning experience. I gave him the card when he was finished and he asked if he could read it there. I said yes, and he read it. He was a stern individual, who had not shared much about his personal life until that moment.

After reading the card, he looked up and said thank you. He proceeded to tell me that he was a father of three, and life had been rough for his wife and children. He shared that the air force represented a new start for them, and it was so important to him to pass this course and provide a different type of life for his wife and kids. He wanted them to be proud of him. He said my card gave him the encouragement to keep focused on his goals, even in moments of self-doubt.

I had a lot of great students over my almost four years as an instructor in the air force. However, I can't remember graduation day for any of them except this student. I remember him holding back tears and having a huge smile on his face when he received his graduation certificate. He shared with me after the ceremony that my words stayed with him each time he took a test or progress check and that it felt good to know someone believed in him and was in his corner through the experience. I was so thankful I gave him that thank-you card. I wholeheartedly believe he would have passed the course without my card, but it may have made the experience just a little easier or more enjoyable for him.

I have had experience after experience like this over the years as a leader because I have made gratitude a part of my life. It connects to my purpose in life: to help others grow and develop and inspire them to take action. I do it for them, but I must say, it has a huge impact on me as well, and it can for you too.

Make gratitude a habit.

New, healthy, helpful habits like gratitude can be hard to form. Below I have outlined three strategies for making gratitude a routine part of your life.

1. Identify your purpose.

The benefits won't come if gratitude is simply a "check the box" exercise because you are reading about how beneficial it can be. The same applies for anything discussed in this book. You have to connect what you are doing to why you are doing it or the exercises will simply be meaningless ones you won't fully embrace. Knowing the purpose behind giving gratitude to others helps keep it a priority when pieces of our life start to shift. On days when we are tired and thinking about skipping or putting off writing thank-you notes, for example, if we connect back to our purpose, we are able to push through the thoughts of skipping out and move to action. I've learned to remind myself that I never know how important my thank-you note may be to someone else. It is important to me (my why) to make sure they know how much I appreciate a particular behavior or action.

I remember a former team member early on in my career who didn't appear to be the most sentimental person. One day though, I was talking about the importance of thank-you cards with her, and I noticed her interest rise in the conversation. I felt curious about this because I honestly didn't think she really appreciated the process. She had never discussed giving out thank-you cards or any type of reward or recognition, nor had she ever shared the impact of receiving them. As our conversation went on, though, she asked me, "Can I share something with you about thank-you cards that is personal to me but ask you to please not share with others on the team?" I obliged, wondering where this share was going.

She was sitting at her desk, and I had been standing during the conversation. She opened her top desk drawer and reached in. When her hand reappeared, there looked to be at least twenty-five to thirty thank-you cards in it. "I've kept every thank-you card I've received in my career," she said. "Oftentimes, when I am having a tough day or up against a barrier and trying to break through creatively, I will go and grab a few of these. I read through them and it helps me remember why I do what I do. I remember that it doesn't go unnoticed. I remember that I get to make an impact, maybe not every day, but oftentimes I do. Many of those times weren't on significant days for me, but others were watching, and it was significant to them. Thank-you cards mean a lot to me!"

I was astonished by this interaction. Here, sitting before me, was a person who I didn't think cared one way or the other about the gratitude of others. However, the impact thank-you notes had on her was clear. I also learned how important practicing gratitude was to her a year later. I had just helped her in a crunch with a large project to ensure it came in on deadline. To me, helping was being a good team member. To her, I found, it meant a lot more. I walked into my office a few days after the project and there on my desk was a meaningful, handwritten thank-you card along with my favorite baked goods. These weren't just any run-of-the-mill baked goodies. I had told the team my favorite line of baked good products, which were only available in a few areas of the United States. Where we were living at the time, we couldn't get them. My team member had hunted down an online recipe for them and made them from scratch as a thank-you! To this day, it is one of the most meaningful moments of gratitude I have experienced, and it has stayed with me well over a decade later. Those from-scratch baked goods were far better than the store-bought ones—both in taste and sentiment.

Moments like these happen when purpose is identified in our gratitude. Special memories are built. Meaningful connections are made. Connect to your purpose for practicing gratitude and you will be surprised by what it can do and how it can impact someone else's life.

2. Practice.

Like with building any habit that adds value to your life, it takes practice before it starts becoming a norm. Have you ever had a workout routine? I really love the programs that are structured in ninety-day periods. The people who truly dedicate themselves to the full ninety days tend to have great success, not just with the program, but also with maintaining a new norm after the ninety days are up. These programs aren't built as quick fixes but instead have you build progress over time. According to research from a team at the University College London, it takes sixty-six days for something to become a habit or what I like to call a lifestyle change. Growing into the habit of gratitude is no different.

So many connect to awareness as the source of improvement in serving or leading others. Awareness is great, but it rarely leads to consistent action. It takes practice to build routines and habits. With gratitude, it may seem disingenuous to have reminders on your calendar to share gratitude with others, but let's examine this for a moment. I have built a habit of writing in "Notes" on my phone when I want to share gratitude with someone. I established this practice because so often the moments of gratitude come during a team meeting or a presentation, when the moment isn't ideal to provide sincere gratitude and lift someone up. I don't want to lose what I felt in that moment, though, and I want to be able to be specific when I share the gratitude with that person. I capture the moment in my notes quickly and continue to work to be fully present. Usually, I have to go from that interaction immediately to another and another as my day continues forward. In order to ensure I take this practice, which has gone somewhat beyond awareness in writing it down, to full-on action, I have gone a step further and created two different times in my weekly calendar for gratitude. During those times, I will write out thank-you cards, maybe order a book that I want to give the person as part of the thank-you. At times, I've called the local bakery or edible food arrangements to order a special gift. I don't find the fact that I've blocked time to do this disingenuous because I want to make it meaningful. I use this time to go back through any notes I've made since the last scheduled time. Sometimes I'll take that time to send the person an invite to go out for lunch and give them the thank-you card I wrote while at lunch. Other times, I drop the thank-you cards at the post office to be mailed to people's homes. The key is that this is a habit for me that took practice. I had to find out what worked for me to be able to connect back to my purpose and share meaningful gratitude consistently. How can you practice the habit? It may be different than my approach. In talking with many others, I've found they often mention journaling.

3. Keep a journal.

Have you ever journaled? I have, and guess what? It takes time. It is not a practice that I've been consistent about. What I've found, though, is that when I am consistent, I am in a higher state of gratitude. I notice more about my day, week, and month, and that gives me a change in perspective. I find that I assume more positive intent in others when I journal. One advantage of this practice is that you don't need much to get started. You can use a laptop, maybe a pencil and paper, or a small notebook. The tricky part is how to embed it into your routine.

Start out by committing to a time of day to write down what you are grateful for. If you feel you have time each morning when you wake up, keep a pen and paper on the nightstand and journal first thing. Take a moment to reflect on how powerful this new habit could be. Instead of doing what many, including myself, often do as soon as their eyes open, which is grab their phones and scroll the news or social media, you will grab your journal and start your day in gratitude. Of course, journaling right before you go to sleep is another option, especially if it takes you a while to fall asleep. This would never work for me. When I hit the bed, I am out!

Set a goal of journaling about one grateful thing a day for the first thirty days. Then two a day for days thirty-one to sixty. And finally, in the home stretch of hardwiring the habit in days sixty-one to ninety, go with three a day. As you grow the habit of journaling your gratitude, evolve the process in ways that are meaningful to you. A big recommendation I'll give in keeping a gratitude journal is to be specific. Specificity means so much more. Get in the practice of doing this with yourself so you can carry it over into giving gratitude to those you lead.

One of the biggest takeaways about gratitude I remember was from an interaction with a team member I once led. I had sent a thank-you card to her home on Monday and she must have received it in the mail on Wednesday. On Thursday morning she walked into my office and said, "I don't know how you do it, but you always know when I need a pick-me-up, and you always say the right things, whether it's in speech or written down!"

The truth was, I didn't always know when or what to say. I did practice showing gratitude regularly, though, and I was always specific in what I was showing gratitude for. When we are specific, people connect to the appreciation in a more real way. It takes them to a moment that meant something to them and helps them see how it meant something to you too. It builds a unique connection of caring and is so much more powerful than just a thank-you.

Asking Questions

So far, I have focused on strong ego management and gratitude practices as two key ways Peaceful Powered Leaders build people up. Now I turn to the third and final way to lift up others. Peaceful Powered

Leaders share their knowledge not by giving answers, but by asking questions.

Today, we seem to have answers at our fingertips to every question. A few key words typed into a search engine and so many potential answers appear that it would take hours to sift through them all. What's become even more valuable than answers is the ability to ask better questions. Questions that make people think, feel, and, in some cases, grow. A big reason for disengagement in the workplace is when leaders have set up an environment where asking questions is looked down upon.

Employees are taught that if you show up, do your job, and get the needed results, you are a good employee. This is a very finite mindset. Notice there is nothing in that definition about being an engaged employee or an employee who seeks new questions or to take on new goals. Most people want to be challenged in the workplace. They want to explore, be creative, and press through new problems, even with the risks of sailing the seas of uncertainty, to get to an outcome they weren't sure they could reach. They don't want someone else sailing the ship, keeping them confined to their specified area day after day. That doesn't allow them to be built up or to grow. This is a hard concept for many leaders to grasp.

Over the years, as a coach and consultant, I've had numerous leaders challenge me on the practice of asking questions over giving answers. Let's explore this approach the way I have with many of them. Leaders tend to believe that having knowledge is more important than asking questions. My question to them is: "Although being knowledgeable got you here, how will it help grow those you serve as a leader?" Isn't that why we are in leadership, to serve others? Or is our purpose of being a leader to get accolades and be in control? From my experience, when we are striving toward a place of external control, it is hard to find a place of inner peace.

Great leaders understand that effective leadership doesn't come from having the control but from setting up an environment where others can step into empowerment and own their situations. Great leaders put the power in the hands of those they lead and accept the consequences—great, good, or bad—from the outcomes. They own the whole process and model this for those they lead, but it isn't through control or power. It is instead through lifting others up and teaching them that having an answer to give them is far less impactful than having questions to ask them.

Leaders have learned that posing questions to those they lead provides a door to growth that telling them answers does not. While asking questions may take more time in the short term, it helps create a different reality for all involved in the future. Let's examine the power of questioning by looking at some specific benefits it provides.

Benefit 1 – Asking questions allows us to find out more about those we lead.

When we ask someone a question, we have the opportunity to listen to how the person responds. We get to listen to their thought process as they share with us, piece by piece, an answer or as they give us one big summary. We get to find out about how they approach a problem. Sometimes they give details about something working well for them we didn't know about or barriers in their way they didn't realize we could help move.

We also find out more and more about their communication style. This is a key piece in being able to flex our style as communicators to better connect with those we lead. The more I've listened to others and been able to flex my style to better complement theirs, the more engaged they became with the questions I asked. This accommodating isn't always easy to do, because sometimes the communication style someone prefers is not natural for me. At times I feel like am venturing to an attic up some rickety steps. I know how to get there, and have a reason for going there, but I don't feel confident about using those stairs. What I remember in those moments, though, is that what might lie in that attic could open a range of possibilities for the person. While it may cause some initial discomfort for me, I'd rather the other person be more comfortable as I flex to meet them where they are. You may ask, "Is it truly genuine if we are flexing our style from our natural approach for someone else?" My answer to that is a wholehearted, "Yes!" As a leader, whether formal, informal, titled, or not, we have the privilege to explore with others in unique ways. This involves asking questions that potentially get better and better over time, because we care enough about the person to find an approach that connects best with them. We are demonstrating care and consideration.

Benefit 2 – Asking questions allows us to engage with those we lead in new ways.

Whether we know the answer or not, posing a question to someone creates the opportunity to dialogue. We may find that a different answer than we expected opens the door to partnering in a new process. Sometimes, when we ask questions, others won't have an answer right away. That is great! We now have engaged their thought process. We have the opportunity to see how they handle not knowing and seeking to find an answer. It allows for stimulation in multiple ways. Additionally, asking questions and truly listening to the answers, and working to partner in implementation of those answers, shares with those we lead that we value them and what they have to say.

Benefit 3 – Asking questions allows for development.

When our team must find an answer without their leader giving it to them, they gain a deeper sense of purpose. They must own the answer and their part in it. This approach creates an environment of curiosity that could potentially lead to new forms of innovation and development. As people seek answers, they often find more areas to explore. With exploration, people often develop knowledge of new approaches that allow them to take action in different ways.

◇

This part of becoming a Peaceful Powered Leader is one of my favorites. Each day in my life that I have the opportunity to build others up is a great day. The rewards I receive are quietly shared appreciation from those I help and seeing people grow. I rarely get public credit for coaching, and I'm great with that. I don't need, and really don't want, my role on public display.

As I write, a newer leader comes to mind who I had the opportunity to coach heavily in her first year in a leadership role. By the end of the year, she was on multiple executives' radars because of her ability to produce results, both in business and with people. She didn't produce results by directing or telling. She built others up, and her team got the results. She didn't catch the eye of the executives at first. I encouraged them to seek her out and explore what she was doing in her department. They quickly saw what I had seen. This leader was doing amazing things *with* her team, and the results were well outside the norm.

When I met her, she wanted to understand what a great leader looked like. As her coach, I didn't give answers. I asked questions and helped guide her to areas she wanted to grow in. She did the work, she applied the learnings, and she got amazing results. To this day, as far as I know, no one knows I coached her. I am happy about that. I am only a small part in her journey, and I'm thankful to be a part of it and don't need any credit for it. My desire is to continue to build her up and watch how she grows and how the impact she has on others' lives expands.

She's the type of person who has the ability to be a CEO, and she's the type of CEO I'd be honored to follow and partner with. I share this to remind you not to only look at where people are now as you strive to build them up, but to also look at where people can be when you choose to build them up consistently. You may play a key role in helping them move past limiting beliefs as they seek to reach new heights in their lives.

Thought Leader Perspective – Nataly Kogan

Nataly Kogan is founder of Happier.com and author of Happier Now: How to Stop Chasing Perfection and Embrace Everyday Moments (Even the Difficult Ones) and Gratitude Daily. *You can learn more at LinkedIn: Nataly Kogan; IG: @natalykogan.*

Narlock: A big piece of your work discussed in your book *Happier Now* is how the ability to be unhappy is crucial to being happier. Why do you feel embracing all types of emotions, even unhappy ones, is essential?

Kogan: One of the things I am truly and very intentionally on a path to ask people is to redefine what it is they mean by happiness or emotional health. My journey is a very personal one in that I held certain perceptions of what it means to be happy for almost forty years. In retrospect [these perceptions] led to my complete and total burnout but were also my way to actually achieving emotional health.

One of those perceptions is very well-ingrained in us by our culture: this idea of happiness as being positive all the time. This is absolutely what I believed and is absolutely normal. We hear all the time "Turn the negative into the positive," "Find the silver lining," and "Turn that frown upside down." Especially in the United States, we live in this culture where there are certain emotions that when we feel them, we think we should find a way out of them as quickly as possible. Research shows exactly the opposite though.

For example, research shows that the people who experience the greatest variety of emotions over their lifetime have higher life satisfaction. Think about that! I remember reading that piece of research early on in my own journey and it just stunned me. The reason for this is that these people have a fuller life experience. They aren't spending their lives trying to avoid a certain feeling, because that takes a tremendous amount of energy.

I try not to use the words "negative" and "positive" with emotions. I try to use the words "easier" and "more difficult" just to get out of that mindset that there is some emotion that is negative, like sadness or worry. Sadness was a big one for me for many years. I was afraid that if I let myself feel it when it came up, I would get stuck in it forever. In fact, research shows this is a very common fear, that most of us, when something difficult happens in our life, dramatically overestimate how bad we will feel and for how long.

We all have this fear that if we just feel the difficult emotion, I'll just use sadness as an example, that we'll get stuck in it forever, that it will never get better. In fact, research shows, and in my own experience of having the gift of teaching this to tens of thousands of people, we must allow ourselves to experience the difficult emotions.

What do I mean by we allow ourselves? I mean that we don't try to escape it. We all have our little escape hatches: Netflix, running, eating too much, drinking too much, social media. We all know what they are, but if we just allow ourselves to feel the emotion, research shows we get through it with less intensity and in a shorter amount of time. That is because we aren't wasting all of this valuable emotional energy trying not to feel something. It takes a lot of energy to try to not feel an emotion. So when we simply allow ourselves the opportunity to feel it, we aren't wasting all this energy. Not only does this allow us to move through that emotion faster, but it also allows us to have more energy available to say, "Okay, this is how I feel. What is the best way I can serve myself right now? What is the best thing I can do, given this is how I feel?"

What I'm talking about is acceptance. This is the first skill: acceptance. We realize that accepting both how things are and how we feel is the opposite of being passive and being stuck. It actually allows us to be in the driver's seat. Then, we can say, "Okay, this is how I feel. What is the best thing I can do to serve myself, to serve the situation, to serve my team?"

I did not have a eureka moment. I didn't learn this easily, and I want to always be really upfront. I completely burnt out, was in a very scary place, and was an absolute terrible leader to my team because I was so overwhelmed with so much doubt, fear, and anxiety. I had never given myself permission to feel these feelings. My coping mechanism was withdrawal. I became this leader who withdrew. I had very few personal conversations with my team because I didn't want to be found out. I put on this very positive front, almost overdoing it, and the cost of that was I was not only making my difficult experience harder, but I wasn't serving my team the best way. My team, of course, realized I was feeling something I didn't want them to know. They then adopted the same behavior. They started to not tell me how they felt. They also started not to tell me about decisions I was making that they didn't agree with.

So, in retrospect, what I would do is say, "Okay, I feel really overwhelmed. What is the best thing I can do right now given this is how I feel? To serve myself, to serve my team, and to serve the moment." What I would say is, "Hey, I need some time off. I'm really not at my best and should not be making decisions." The second thing is I would share that with the team. And this is what I do now. My colleague and I now practice this skill regularly in person. If there is something going on in my day that is stressful or difficult, when I talk with her, I'll start out by letting her know, "Hey, there is something on my mind, so if I'm a little short or something, this is what is going on."

I'm allowing myself to feel how I feel, and I'm being open about that, which then fosters openness. I'm sharing some of my experiences and the research with it because it is so powerful to learn how to be okay with not being okay. Acceptance, as I define it, is shifting from judgment to clarity. It's learning to look at how you feel, not from a place of judgment, saying, "This is how I should feel," but instead from a place of clarity, "This is how I feel." I'm not asking anyone to like feeling sad or frustrated. Those are not fun things to feel, but that is exactly what clarity is. Judgment is liking or not liking how we feel.

The skill of acceptance is the first skill I teach and the first skill I talk about because without it, we are really, really stuck. It is a skill of being able to look at how things are and how you feel with clarity instead of judgment and using that not as your period at the end of a sentence but as your starting point to ask, "What is the best thing I can do right now given how I feel?" The research is there and my experience is there. This is one of the most powerful things we can do as people and as leaders. It is to shift how we think of happiness away from being positive all the time and toward the fact that true emotional well-being means that we learn how to embrace all of our emotions, including the difficult ones.

Narlock: From a leadership perspective, how do you believe your work around happiness can help a leader if it's applied to serve those on their teams better?

Kogan: I think there are a couple of really specific things. One of the core discoveries for me, and this is a big focus of what I do now, is to discuss that emotional health is a leadership skill. It is one of the core leadership skills. This is because as a leader, and I know I'm not alone, I thought my emotional well-being belonged right at the bottom of the list because first comes my team. I was in this idea that I need to take care of them and put myself at the bottom. I think there are so many leaders who operate this way. Even leaders who understand emotion still do this martyr leadership because they care so much about their team.

In fact, though—I share this at the end of my talks—you cannot give what you don't have. It is not possible at all, under any circumstances, however special you may be, and I definitely have my arguments with this in my head. You cannot be a great leader if you are suffering, if you are struggling, if you feel overwhelmed, and if you are not aware of your emotions. If you are not practicing your own emotional health as a skill, you cannot help your team.

I was doing some research, and the research is really scary and also inspiring. As a leader, we have a thousand times—a million times—greater impact than anyone else. So if your leader is bringing their stress to work, they can actually impact your heart health. There is research showing this. I work with leaders all the time who are wonderful human beings, and they care so much about their teams, and they are actually hurting their teams very much because they are not taking care of themselves. One of the biggest leadership skills that we aren't teaching in MBA programs and aren't teaching in leadership programs is that your emotional health as a leader is a leadership skill. Without it, you cannot bring your best and help your people bring their best.

With leaders who model sustainable well-being and sustainable work, their people on their teams double their well-being, and they double their productivity. Think about that!

As leaders, the most essential piece is a mind shift away from martyr leadership and toward emotionally healthy leadership, where you as a leader are practicing your emotional health as a skill. Culture is just the emotional health of a team. So, you cannot have an emotionally healthy culture and team if, as a leader, you aren't practicing this yourself.

Chapter 3

Peaceful Powered Leaders Put Service to Others Ahead of Service to Self

I was a communications computer systems instructor in the United States Air Force. I achieved the rank of E-5, or Staff Sergeant, before deciding to separate, and I was honorably discharged from my military service. While in the air force, I was taught the core values of "Integrity first," "Service before self," and "Excellence in all we do." For a long time, I struggled with the core value of service before self because I didn't understand during my military service what it meant. I think there were a lot of leaders around me who fell into this bucket too, mostly because people interpreted the value based on military stereotypes.

A running air force joke was that the military didn't issue you a family. This saying was so prevalent because people took "service before self" to mean the military comes ahead of your personal desires, including your family. This is the stereotype many of us held of military service. I always struggled with this because I greatly valued my family, and although I was serving my country, it was still a job and I put my family above it. It wasn't until years later that I truly understood what this core value meant and how powerful it was in becoming a Peaceful Powered Leader.

A person is not ready to peacefully lead others until they have released self-service in exchange for serving others. When this is really accomplished, a leader can act in accordance with their values to care for, stand up for, grow, and nourish those they lead without fear of what happens to self. It doesn't mean they can't or don't take care of themselves. It means they have healthy ego management and understand that the needs of the whole may need to come before their personal desires or what they'd prefer at times. So often people want to lead but allow self-preservation to come before serving others. It hinders their actions to make the tough decision and, usually, the right one.

Have you ever heard a person share a story that made you gasp? In the moment, you think, "I'd never do that. There is no way I would react or respond that way." If you are human, like me, you've probably had the experience of acting in a way that didn't reflect your values. For me, one of these instances concerned a bonus. I was on a team that was months away from receiving bonuses. Some of the target goals had already been hit, including the one I was in charge of. It felt like at almost every meeting we had, the overall topic of discussion was the goals, but the story I told myself was that the underlying concern was really the bonuses. While we had to hit certain goals to get parts of the bonus, the whole bonus was tied to meeting financial outcomes. If we didn't make our budget targets, then we didn't get any bonus, regardless of what other goals had been met. Sure, the goals were good for the organization and had positive intent, but I told myself that most people in the room truly cared most about the bonus, including myself. It was a potentially large payout and not something I had experienced before.

There we sat, in the last quarter of the fiscal year. We were close to hitting the budget goal, but if we didn't execute just right, we were going to miss it and the bonuses. The talk was about what cost-saving measures we could implement. The budget I was in charge of was well under, and I had already made the significant cuts I was asked to.

Thankfully, I had an innovative team, and they helped make the cuts without significant impact to our customers. The one large thank-you for them for reaching that goal was getting to go on an educational trip. I was excited that the majority of the team was going to be able to go to different learning conferences over the last few months of the fiscal year. It was something they were looking forward to since we had budgeted for it before the start of that fiscal year. As we leaders sat around the table going over further cost-cutting measures, one person, who still had a large budget deficit, brought up education travel. He shared that while he had cut all travel for his teams, he had heard others were still traveling.

Immediately, the majority of the room latched on to this discussion, echoing the idea that we must cut travel through the rest of the fiscal year. I sat, trying to rapidly think about how to address this, while being deliberate in ensuring the frustration I had on the inside wasn't coming through on the outside. At first, I went to blame. Instead of assuming positive intent and withholding judgment, I blamed the leader for bringing up this suggestion. I then went to blaming others for going along with the suggestion. I knew that cutting travel for the last fiscal quarter was not going to make a huge impact in the overall deficit that needed to be made up. I knew my team was looking forward to these opportunities and had worked hard for them. I also knew that, if I spoke up, I was potentially going to put myself in the minority opinion of the conversation. I knew I could very quickly be labeled by the team as not being a team player. I also knew my own team would ultimately understand. Lastly, I knew I wanted the bonus, and in that moment, I thought about serving myself over others in more ways than one. I stepped out of leadership and into self-preservation.

I didn't speak up or push back in the discussion about cutting the education travel budget for the final quarter. I did what was easy over what felt right. My own team members grew in multiple ways each time they got to go on an investment trip like these learning conferences. What they would have brought back and worked to implement, based on previous conferences, would have paid far greater dividends than the few thousand dollars we'd be saving for that short moment in time. Again, though, I didn't speak up. The decision was made that the travel education budget would be cut for everyone for the rest of the fiscal year.

I left the room and immediately went to talk in person to those impacted. As I knew they would be, they were understanding. I shared how the decision applied to all and how it was going to help the organization. I could see the looks of sadness on their faces. To have their travel approved, each one had to share with me why they wanted to go to a particular conference and what they planned to bring back to the organization from their learning. I remembered them eagerly describing those details as I shared the disappointing news that none of them would be going. What I didn't share with them, though, was that I hadn't spoke up once to respectfully debate the topic on the floor of that meeting. I had not worked to set and own my reality and, consequently, I was not in peace in the moment. I served the comfort of myself at that meeting. I told myself I was being a team player and that I was putting the organization first and working toward the greater good of the whole. I reminded myself that we still had to meet budget targets and were accountable to our board for doing so, and I was helping with that. All of that was true. I also convinced myself that the rest of the room of leaders was thinking the way I was, that they wanted their bonuses too, and if it meant sacrificing short-term, they'd do it, just like I was doing. At least that was the story I told myself because I had no way of knowing that for sure. I chose comfort for myself over investment in those I was leading and their growth and development. I blamed the person who spoke up about the idea in the first place, and, in my mind, I threw insults at the type of leader he was because he had a large budget deficit. The truth, though, was that leader was probably doing the best he could, and I hadn't stepped up or spoken up for what I felt was right and important. The only person responsible was me because I didn't even try. As I reflected on how I had allowed myself to do this, I realized I was missing connection to some essential values that had gotten me to the current leadership role I was in. My sights were set on goals that weren't connected to my values, and, before I knew it, my values weren't truly values but simply recommendations to consider and discard if they didn't fit nicely into the needed outcome or easier decision.

Like this story of the bonus, the budget, and the service to myself over others, one of my other biggest failures in leadership is the story I already shared in the introduction about payday. In that instance, I was so worried about taking care of myself and staying out of potential harm's way with my CEO that I failed to do the right thing for those I led directly, who were on my team, and the other thousands of employees in the organization. In both instances, payday and the travel education budget, I put myself before service to others. Putting service to others in front of service to self means we've *already* made the decision we are going to do what is right ahead of what may be easy or beneficial to ourselves personally.

I remember another time, though, of watching a fellow leader do the opposite of what I had done, and it is a lesson I carry close with me to this day. I was in a meeting with other leaders as we were working to make a decision that was going to impact Human Resources, Supply Chain, and Finance in multiple ways. One choice was much easier for Human Resources and Finance and overall benefitted the organization. That same choice would be a much harder journey for Supply Chain. As the leaders were debating back and forth over the decision, the leader of Supply Chain spoke up. He confidently said, "This choice will not be popular with my team. This choice is going to cause me to step into a difficult road. This choice is not what's right for Supply Chain. It is, however, what is right for the organization as a whole. And because it is right for the organization as a whole, I'm all in for supporting it." And with those words, the debating stopped, the decision was made, and we moved forward.

One selfless act made it so much easier to lead with the right decision. The selfless act didn't please all, but it was the right decision for that moment, and it was a brave choice. How can we, like this Supply

Chain leader, be consistent in choosing service to others over service to self? It truly is a game changer as leaders. Getting there isn't that easy though—or is it?

Learning to lead in peace and choosing service to others over service to self involves three practices that build on each other. Are these the only three things you will need to set your values? Probably not, as each person's journey is different. However, these three practices make a powerful starting point:

1. Connect your leadership to your values.
2. Ensure you walk the path of what's right—which isn't always what's easy.
3. Be a role model in both word and action while building trust.

Now, let's explore each of these three areas and work through some exercises that will allow you to build the foundation for service to others over service to self.

Connect your leadership to your values.

When's the last time you took a step back and wrote your values out on a piece of paper? Chances are the answer is either a long time ago or never. Have you ever shared your values with people close to you or with those you lead? Values are something we talk about in vague ways and describe generally rather than with specifics. We don't often take time to reflect on or evaluate them. We may not be aware that they evolve as we grow or as we talk about them on a regular basis with others. How can we change this? First, we can start by identifying where our values are today. A big piece of this exploration process is ensuring we narrow our values down and get away from the catchall and vagueness that often comes with discussing values. We talk about the values we want to be known for but those often aren't our true values. I'll share an example of this contradiction, which involves my faith.

I am a person who believes in God. Many would classify me as a Christian. I share that I am a Christian with others; however, that word,

Christian, has taken on various meanings in religious circles. I have thought a lot about changing how I share my beliefs. Today, I would say I am a person of faith who believes in God. I have a relationship with God, and it is not where I'd like it to be because I haven't invested in the relationship the way I know I have in other strong relationships I have.

That relationship is between God and me. I may talk about it with others, but it is ultimately between the two of us. My beliefs aren't all associated with a particular religion or denomination. As I share this, I want to say that in my heart, a top-three value of mine is faith in God, and that value guides my decision-making, but I know right now that it isn't. This is a hard realization for me. However, if we can identify our values, even though what we find might disappoint us, we can then strengthen as well as change them if they aren't in alignment with who we want to be. Knowing our values is a key piece of being a Peaceful Powered Leader. This knowledge makes it so much easier to make the tough decisions that truly are in alignment with our values and to not think twice about them. When we know and have strong connection to our values, decisions we make don't rumble over and over in our brains. We own them and their outcomes and move forward peacefully.

So how can you identify your values? Let's discuss the process before going through the exercise.

Identifying our values is so vital. Our values, in a sense, are our brand. They are how many people identify us. They play a big role in guiding our decision-making, and they help define who we are and what we will and won't do. So often, though, people are timid about sharing their values for fear of what others may think, say, or believe. This is a problem in our thought process and will be a barrier to serving others in lieu of serving ourselves. We can serve others in a way that doesn't compromise our values and be true to ourselves by holding true to how we define ourselves.

Ensure you walk the path of what's right—which isn't always what's easy.

So often, we confuse pleasing others with serving others. We compromise our values to please people who are asking us to do something that goes against our brand—what we stand for. I've failed in this way many times; however, I have an example of when I stood firm and true to my values because they were clearly defined and connected to what I was doing.

I was once asked by an executive to report on coaching conversations I was having with leaders in the organization. Complying with what he asked of me would be a huge compromise. First, my coaching certification carried with it a strong code of ethics that held to confidentiality between those I was coaching and myself. This executive was asking me to break that code of ethics. The executive asked me to update him on achievements, areas of concern, and how I felt individuals were progressing.

When I start coaching relationships with people, I discuss what coaching is and isn't. I discuss our relationship and work to set a strong foundation built on trust. One of the key pieces I share is that I'm there to help guide them to the growth and development outcomes they are striving for. I have had people share their fears, their failures, their successes, their triumphs, and so much more. People open themselves, becoming vulnerable in these sessions in an attempt to grow.

What this executive was asking me to do was to place pleasing him over serving those I committed to helping honorably and over holding firm to both my values and the code of ethics associated with my coaching certification. I was nervous to tell this executive no but knew I couldn't compromise. I valued being a coach and having a clear conscious about not compromising people's trust and honoring relationships and my value of connectedness. Being true to these values was a huge part of being at peace. The executive wasn't happy with my decision but ultimately knew he had asked something he shouldn't have and didn't push the issue. I know this wasn't the guaranteed outcome, and I could've lost my role in the company and a big portion of my financial income. But I would have been at peace with that because I made a decision that connected to my values.

Knowing Your Personal Values Exercise

Knowing your personal values helps set patterns of behavior. I questioned for a while why that executive thought it was okay to ask me what he did. I realized I was inconsistent at times because I hadn't actually sat down and done the work to clearly define my values. So, I went to work. Here's the process I used, and have used with others, that has proven effective.

1. Start with questions, not answers.

When it comes to our values, we think we already know the answers. As I shared previously, I thought one of my answers would be my faith. Through this questioning process, however, I realized that while my faith is something I value, it isn't as strong of a value as I want it to be. So, with this exercise, regardless of what you think your values are or how strong you consider them, come to the exercise with a fresh slate and an open mind. Let's start with the following four questions. Take time to write out your answers and be specific, providing examples and details.

- *What particular situations from your life have brought out the most emotion in you?* Consider both comfortable, or easy, emotions and uncomfortable, or difficult, emotions.
- *What events or actions have you taken that you are most proud of? How would you describe yourself when you feel you are at your best?*
- With this question, remember to stay in reality and focus on when *you* feel *you* are at your best, not when you feel *others* think you are at your best. The process and exploration are for you. There are no judgments here.
- *What process do you use to make hard choices or decisions?*

2. Identify your purpose in life.

I've worked with many people who were unhappy in one area of their lives. Some were not satisfied with their job. Others were upset about their partnership or marriage. Several people revealed being frustrated with volunteer work they did. But whatever they were upset about, the majority of people had not explored why. They hadn't taken the time to find a root cause because they thought they already knew the answer. As some of them committed the time to explore why they were unhappy, they found that the area they were upset, struggling, or frustrated in didn't reflect their values. Here are some examples.

A person upset with her job was being asked to produce metrics that compromised the way she took care of people. Caring for others was closely aligned with one of her top three values. She didn't approach her leader about it, though, and loved the team she worked with and wasn't looking for changes.

A man struggled in his marriage because his partner asked him to regularly put a type of persona on around family and friends and wasn't open to discussing the frustration he had with this. It was compromising his values, and upon self-reflection, he discovered he was spending more and more time at work to avoid, not his partner, but not living his values. At work he could connect to who he was and this made it a happier place for him.

A woman continued to volunteer at a center she had been a part of in various ways for years. She started in a particular area she was passionate about, but as she volunteered more and more frequently, leaders at the center moved her to a different area that wasn't connected to what she was passionate about. She was upset but didn't want to say anything because she felt thankful for the opportunity to help in general.

In each of these three cases, people shared with me how they were upset, but they hadn't reflected on why to the point of making an actionable change. They associated their frustrations with a person rather than with not owning the situation and the opportunity to change it. This is common when we aren't leading our thoughts with our values.

Our values can be our guiding star if we choose to put in the time, effort, and energy to identify them and then bring them into our thought process regularly. They can help us own our reality versus blaming others. They can guide us to serve others in a way that deeply connects with who we are, versus in a way that is simply to please.

I share these examples to help stimulate thought for you on how you can own your purpose in life. My purpose in life is to help people grow, develop, and inspire others to take action. With my purpose, and my values guiding that purpose, it has become much easier and more peaceful for me to make decisions without second-guessing or thinking about the "what-ifs."

Take some time and think about the areas in your life right now that you feel you thrive in and why. What are the areas in your life you are struggling in and why? Again, be specific and deliberate in how you identify these areas. Write it all out and, when you are finished, move to question three.

3. What words connect to your purpose and how do they define you?

Go back through your answers so far for this exercise and look for words that appear several times and point to themes. What are the words that jump out at you because they connect to you, resonate with you? Additionally, go through and search out words, particularly in your answers to question two of the exercise, that contradict the key words you identified as feeling connected to. What was different in those instances that you felt disconnected? What would it have looked like if you were fully owning the situation? How could you have taken action differently?

As you work through this process, I want you to nail down your top three values. That's it! So many people struggle with values because they have six or eight or ten or eleven or more of them, and they have so many because they haven't truly nailed them down. I shared the story about my faith because it is an example of something that is in my top five, but it isn't truly a 100 percent firm value. It is what I want but not where I am right now or what I value most right now. I want that to change, and I can work on that, but it's not there. My top three, though, they are firm, and I honestly am not that happy about one of them because it in some ways contradicts the faith value. I want to work to make that change, and I can own doing that.

If you are looking through the words and are struggling to nail down the ones that really resonate, below is a list of commonly used value words for assistance. Challenge yourself, though, to choose words that you feel good about. A word may not be easy for others to understand or enticing, but this exercise is for you, not others. Some have shared with me how they chose a word from the list below that appeared in their answers because it was easier for them to explain to others. But when they talked about the word, it didn't bring forth the true passion and value of the word that truly resonated with them in this exercise.

Again, these are *your* values. It is important to share and talk about them with your team and others in your life, especially in extending or growing trust, but don't let that hinder the word choice. Once you've identified your three values, or maybe just two or one, celebrate them! Celebrate knowing you took the time to discover why these values mean so much to you. Start thinking about how you will incorporate them into your decision-making moving forward and how you can be consistent with that. The next part of the exercise on trust can help with this process.

Values List			
(In no particular order and not exhaustive.)			
Integrity	Respect	Teamwork	Innovation
Trust	Diversity	Accountability	Openness
Awareness	Empathy	Happiness	Fun
Faith	Humility	Balance	Resiliency
Boldness	Peacefulness	Security	Creativity

Serenity	Thoughtfulness	Harmony	Exploration
Determination	Persuasive	Calmness	Respectful
Acceptance	Encouragement	Fair	Precise
Gratitude	Dependability	Passion	Ethical
Strength	Healthy	Energetic	Commitment
Leadership	Spontaneous	Rational	Bold
Adaptable	Purposeful	Discipline	Growth
Patience	Mastery	Sincerity	Elegant
Compassion	Encouragement	Risk	Learning
Service	Reliability	Joyful	Connection
Transparent	Nurturing	Adventurous	Warm
Wisdom	Courage	Genuine	Approachable
Optimism	Uniqueness	Loyalty	Success

Model your values for others in both word and action while building trust.

When it comes to serving others, before serving self, it is vital the path we walk matches the words we say. In leaning in to and owning being a Peaceful Powered Leader, you will build trust with others as well as yourself. Identifying your values is an essential piece because they are the guiding light for us in both word and action. It is one thing to say we'll support someone, and another to take the action to do it. Doing both has the power to build strong, trusting relationships. Now that you know your top three values, let's jump into the next piece.

Let's examine what trust looks like, how it is built, both with ourselves and others, and how it can be lost. I'll reference the work of Stephen M. R. Covey here, the author of *The Speed of Trust*. Mr. Covey found in his research that trust is made up of equal parts character and competence. He found that trust is often built through competence, which is partly defined as following through in action on what we say we are going to do. Think about that for a moment and how strongly follow-through relates to both our self-trust and growing trust with others.

How many times have you said you were going to start something but didn't? Not only are we personally aware of this, but so are those we shared it aloud with. If we aren't following through, we will start questioning whether we will truly take action whenever we say we will. Additionally, those we shared with are probably going to take notice of our inability to follow through.

On the other end of the spectrum, think about someone who consistently follows through. We don't question them when they say they are going to do something. We also have a sense of peace with their dependability. We know they will follow through because of their track record, and that is a great feeling. Those we lead want to feel this way about us, their leaders. While taking action can build trust, being a person of word but no action can quickly break trust down.

I remember one time in my coaching practice when I worked with a leader who appeared to be far from peace. In an hour-long session I had with her, she shared five different examples of actions she had taken in the past week that didn't match her words. This leader clearly wanted to be a great leader in word but wasn't putting in the work it takes to move words into action.

She shared how she cared about others, their growth and development, their success, and being an example for those she led. She then proceeded to tell me how she had said something extremely hurtful about another leader to one of her team members. And guess what? A direct report of the person she was badmouthing overheard and was shocked and immediately confronted her. What was interesting, and later self-clarifying for the leader sharing with me, is that she wasn't upset at herself for saying what she said but was instead upset she was caught. As she explored why this was, the leader realized she had been on a path that strayed far outside of her values.

The leader discussed how she had lost the trust of her team and her peers. She initially said it was because of this incident. This could've been true, as many violations of trust occur because of violations associated to someone's actions of character, which are usually things said in words. But as this leader explored who she had become, she realized the truth was that she had become a leader who was all over the place when it came to values.

Her leadership was a vast ocean, full of waves of drama. She spoke negatively about those she led, complaining about one team member to another. She didn't actually spend much time helping others grow and develop but instead spent time in drama-filled conversations about the organization she worked for and her leader, as well as those she led. "I've lost my way," she finally said to me, and she broke down in tears.

Our way is guided by our values, and it is easy to lose it when we haven't kept our values front and center as our north star.

I continued to work with this leader as she identified her values and built a plan to regain both others' trust and the peace that came with living her values. I saw a very different person evolve over the next six months as this leader went through some massive discomfort to push herself to grow. She eventually gained back the trust of her peers and those she led and went on to be the leader she had described herself as in our first session—the difference was that this time her words matched her actions.

Examining Our Trust Exercise

Let's pause here and take a moment for you to evaluate yourself in regard to trust. Grab the values you selected in the previous exercise and use them as your guide for this exercise. Below are questions that relate to both others' trust and self-trust. Be honest with yourself as you answer these questions. Don't circle the response you want to be able to give but instead be true in your growth journey and select the response that reflects where you are and where you are going to have to start working from to grow. Keep in mind you can't make anyone trust you, but you can influence them. I've had people go through this exercise and use the opt-out that it is not their fault when they are perceived as an untrustworthy leader; it's the fault of those who won't trust them. Stay in the ownership and accountability mindset we previously explored.

Go through and reflect on each question and your response. Again, there is no judgment about how you answer and no right or wrong choice. The purpose of the exercise is for you to stop and consider where you are. Do you feel your answers show you are in alignment with your values? Do your responses indicate that you are building up or breaking down trust with others and yourself? How do you know the answers involving others are accurate? Do you take time to have open dialogue with trusted coworkers who you know will provide growth feedback? If so, who are those people? Have you identified them? Have you talked with them about the role they play in your life for growth in building trust?

While the questions in the exercise provide you some insight, trust involves being courageous and having dialogue with others in an open, honest, and vulnerable way. It is opening yourself up to hear things that may be hard to hear while assuming they are being shared with positive intent. It is taking that feedback and exploring it even further through self-examination to build upon your internal trust. This exercise and section are simply a starting point, a foundational piece, which you can build on to take further action.

I regularly have conversations with people about the trust in our relationship.

When I first started this, it did catch people off guard. I had to learn to share the why behind the conversation and the what, as in what I promised to do with the information and what I promised not to do with the information. It opened the door to tough conversations that eventually led to a more peaceful state. I didn't let my mind wander over what I thought this person thought about me, or why they made that look or gesture. I trusted what they said and held to my values throughout the process.

As part of this process, I recommend you explore Dr. Brenè Brown's and Stephen M. R. Covey's research on trust. Both of them have dedicated substantial time and energy to the topic. While I am working to set a foundation, their work can help you step into the next levels of growth. I encourage you to go there.

Trust Self-Reflection	
I follow through on items I say I will complete.	Never Sometimes Most of the time Always
I don't talk negatively about others, and if I have constructive feedback to give someone, they are present when I give it.	Never Sometimes Most of the time Always
I celebrate others' success with them and look for opportunities to build others up.	Never Sometimes Most of the time Always
I communicate to others in a way that makes it easy to know where I stand on a particular situation or topic.	Never Sometimes Most of the time Always
I work to ensure others can provide me growth feedback by opening myself up to it and listening to the feedback without intent of rebuttal.	Never Sometimes Most of the time Always
I give my opinion freely to others without concern of their feelings or without facts in the situation.	Never Sometimes Most of the time Always

I meet deadlines that I agree to.	Never Sometimes Most of the time Always
I call, text, email, or respond to others in a consistent manner. (This means if I normally respond within twenty-four hours, I stay consistent in this approach with all.)	Never Sometimes Most of the time Always
I share my learnings, wisdom, and knowledge with others in an open forum.	Never Sometimes Most of the time Always
I set goals for myself and hold myself to achieving them	Never Sometimes Most of the time Always

Trusting ourselves and having the trust of others because of our ability to live in the character and competence of our values is a freeing experience. We don't walk around waiting for the other shoe to drop. Is someone going to find out I can't do this? No, because I was honest about my skills and abilities. Is someone going to find out that I said that about them? No, because I don't talk about others unless they are present, and I can address concerns directly.

You can go on and on asking questions about old worries and fears. If you are living your values and growing trust with yourself and others, your answers will reflect your new peace. Having done the work to connect to your values and live in a way that keeps you true to yourself and others in both word and action makes it easier to serve others over being self-serving.

Employees today in workplaces want to work for their purpose over a paycheck. They'd rather have a leader who invests in them and their development, focusing on helping them grow, than be in a work environment that offers comfort without the push to drive through discomfort toward growth. When employees know they have a leader who is there for them, they can feel it and see it. Peaceful Powered Leaders are connected to their purpose and it drives the way they treat those they lead.

Thought Leader Perspective – David Shove-Brown

David Shove-Brown is a partner and founder of //3877 Design Firm, named in the 50 Best Places to Work in Washington, D.C. Find out more at LinkedIn: David Shove-Brown; IG: @velocityg.

Narlock: What are some ways you focus on investing in your people and how do you feel it impacts their passion for what they do?

Shove-Brown: I think the first and foremost element is honesty. We made it a point from day one that we were going to tell people this is how much money this project is bringing us. This is how much someone owes us. This is how much money something costs. Money was always the thing as an architect and working for other firms that you just didn't talk about. So you didn't know if you were being productive. If you were making money or if someone else was. So we start off with open honesty.

Let's talk about how much it costs to run the office. We don't talk about salaries. We do talk about how we can work more efficiently on a project so we can get a few more dollars so we can have a nicer holiday party, or we can get cool hats, or whatever it is. I think that starts people with the understanding that we are sharing just about everything. What we are sharing is legitimate. It is not just lip service. It is actual, factual information.

I think because money is one of those things that is such a delicate subject, when you start talking about it with your people, they realize, "Holy Crap! These guys are sharing more than other firms I've been at." So that sort of sets the bar. Then you're able to have that conversation with people, and say, "Let's focus on telling people what they are doing really well. And let's tell them what they aren't doing as well and discuss how we can approach it."

I never want to have the mentality of a fear-based workplace. We had an employee screw something up years ago. She forgot to bring drawings to an offsite meeting. [The team] pulled it out. It was fine, it wasn't the end of the world. So we were talking about it later, and she actually feared we were going to fire her. I asked her why I would do that. She shared, "I made us look so stupid." My response was that we pulled it out, and it wasn't a big deal. Then I asked her if she was ever going to do that again, and she replied, "No way." That's even better because now she's looking to help someone else learn from what she did once. It's trying to get people to understand, we are all on the ship together. And I think that starts from honesty.

From there, it's actually hearing people, hearing what they say and how they want to contribute. From their experience working with different bosses, either they will tell you, "Yeah that's a great idea" and do nothing with it, or they would just sort of go, "Okay, carry on." But when you have an open, honest discussion with your team, you can discuss that anyone can have a good idea. And when somebody has a good idea and you implement it, people are like, "Wow, they are actually listening!" And we say, "Yes, if you can find a better way to do something, make the office better, or do this better, let's do it. Come on, let's go." I think that really shows people their value.

It's important to look at investment in different ways. Like turnover—am I losing three or four people a year just because I am a jerk? At some point, you have to have that hard look at yourself. We basically say that anyone who walks in the door, we are probably fifteen to twenty thousand dollars in the hole between computer systems, software, and things like that. The last thing you need to be doing is going and treating them badly, so they take any experience they have and walk out the door. It's a hard thing sometimes to take your ego and put it aside and be like, "Okay, let's look at the big picture. Let's figure this out and work to get the best out of people."

Narlock: Your team has a lot of outings and a lot of celebrations together. What are your thoughts around how these types of interactions connect to how the team feels overall and their engagement and sense of pride in being part of //3877?

Shove-Brown: My business partner and I struggled early on to stop and celebrate success. Sometimes you just get so in the weeds and your foot's on the gas and you are going and going. You feel like you are constantly putting out a fire or dealing with some other problem, and you lose sight of what you've done and what you've accomplished. We tried to work to overcome this cycle. We actually made one of our team members our Minister of Fun!

I don't need to give her permission. I don't need to tell her when to do something. If she sees there's some sort of disturbance in the force and she believes we need donuts in the morning, she just does it. We get reminded that we may need to hit the reset button. Things may have been a little rocky recently, and we sometimes have to come together and remember that as a group we are doing really cool stuff and it also reminds us to keep things in perspective.

While I understand that clients generally have a decent amount of money invested in what we are doing, we aren't curing cancer, and we try to get our clients to realize that things may not go the right direction, or the direction we thought it would go, but we can fix it. We want our employees to realize that sometimes people lose their temper because they don't know how to react in that moment. We want our team to realize that in these moments, it is still okay. We can shake that moment off and keep things in perspective.

We try to do community service outings sometimes. Other times, we'll stop and go to a soccer game together and focus on us all enjoying being together and celebrate that we've done some really great stuff. Sometimes we reflect and together take a hard look at the world around us and say, "What can we do as architecture people and humans to make life just a little bit better?"

We keep perspective on life. We are building buildings and it's cool, but there's a much bigger world out there with much more important things than just that.

Narlock: How do you check in with your team members to ensure they are getting what they need and maintain a shared ownership perspective with what they are working on?

Shove-Brown: You start with open, honest dialogue. People get that and respect that it goes both directions. You establish that open dialogue and the ability for people to come up to you and be okay asking to run something by you or asking to talk about something. When people see that you are supporting them, this helps. We've done things that may seem a little weird. We had a team member a while back, and the apartment she shared with her husband was broken into. One thing stolen was their computer. We bought her a computer. She asked how she could pay it back. We told her you don't pay it back; you do the right thing for the next person. Another person's father got sick and he shared he had to drive to Las Vegas. We let him know we'd buy his plane ticket. We try to remind our team we truly are here to help them, and as we do this, our team realizes we are actual humans who work here, and they want to be a part of that.

We are in the process of bringing on a new team member to help keep my partner's time and my time flexible enough to still be able to walk around the office and see how people are doing or go grab a coffee and ensure we are able to stay focused on establishing those relationships.

Dave, my partner at //3877, and I have been best friends for thirty years, since college. We may have argued twice in our lifetime together. People see that we actually really enjoy being with one another and are challenging each other to do better work. At the end of the day, he makes me laugh hysterically and vice versa. People see that the two people who run the place actually get along really well and have open dialogue. They see this and think, as team members, we should all be able to do that. Our relationship and the way we interact with each other sets a tone for our team. If you tell people we are open to conversation and then push people away when they want to have a conversation, you aren't going to establish openness. You have to establish that brand of openness and let people know you are open to talk.

Narlock: Your company has been named one of the best places to work in Washington, D.C. for numerous years now. I learned that a big piece of that designation comes from the employees who work in the company sharing their feelings about the organization. Why do you feel the employees at //3877 feel this way and how do you think the environment continues to foster these feelings?

Shove-Brown: A lot of people ask us about culture. Leaders want to create culture in an office, but people are smart. You can't just say we are going to create a culture and then not actually create it. People can tell if you are just saying this is our culture and this is what we are going to do. If people feel you aren't doing that, they'll speak up about it.

Employees want to be a part of a place that takes care of people, and that means more than work. When we hire, we look for people who want to be a part of more, who want to buy into that culture. When they get here, we want to encourage that. There are still days that suck; there are days that suck at any job. There are days where I know I have to encourage somebody and help them bring their game face, or days where you know you need to put your arm around that person, and you know they may cry because maybe something just went sideways. You have to know the difference between those things. For us, it is establishing the culture, people buying into it, and us together making it so. We celebrate these awards we've received as a firm. My partner and I aren't ever like, "Look what we created and you guys work for us."

I hate when people at the office introduce me as their boss. We are teammates, that is what we are. We are all working together. I think when you establish that mentality as a team, every dream we have and accomplish is a team victory.

We have a kudos box. I actually stole this idea from one of our clients. When somebody does something that most people don't see, you write it down on a kudos slip and put it in the box. Every Monday morning, we read them together as a team. They are different examples of people sharing how someone helped them. What's really amazing is that people will take the kudos and tape them up around their workstation. It's so awesome. People really respect it and really love it. It helps us celebrate in another way as a team.

Narlock: As one of the leaders in the organization, you've got to make tough decisions at times. How do you get to where you are at a place of peace about the decisions? How do you model that for the team?

Shove-Brown: My partner and I have definitely had to make hard decisions together. We've had employees who didn't work out and clients who didn't work out. We have a lot of conversations together and, through supporting one another, we ask ourselves, what is the best decision for the firm? What's the best decision for the people who are here?

We fired two clients, and it was really hard to do. We have this money coming in and we ask ourselves, "Are we going to take a client that pays us to do what we like to do?" We say yes, but then we evaluate and sometimes realize these are awful people; they just aren't nice. And they are taking it out on us and our team, and we stop and ask, "What's that worth?" When you have the support of the people around you, it makes those decisions easier.

The first time we had to let someone go, I went home and actually cried to my wife. I really liked the person. The person actually went on to a slight career change, much better for them. It is really hard to separate the person from the position. I know that person's spouse. I know their dog. You realize that you've been working with this person and giving them feedback. You've given them baselines to hit and they don't. These are hard decisions to make.

Narlock: Have you been able to reflect on how the team has watched your partner and you make tough decisions and see, as a pretty cool byproduct, how they've stepped up through your model to also make tough decisions?

Shove-Brown Absolutely! It is actually amazing to see. My job is to support our team. In some cases, someone will come to us and say, "I got a situation and can't figure it out. Can you help?" Other times, a client will reach out and share, "I got to tell you what happened onsite. Leslie just knocked it out of the park, and it was amazing." That's when you sit back and realize we are doing what we are trying to do. It's great!

Chapter 4
Peaceful Powered Leaders Invest in Others

W e have focused on how Peaceful Powered Leaders build others up, but a part of this is how they invest in others. This piece of developing as a leader also relates to and extends the foundation of trust we discussed in the previous chapter. Just as you are working to grow as a leader, today's workforce wants to grow and develop too. Gone are the days when organizations put the whole responsibility for employees' learning on the shoulders of their direct leaders. It is now understood in high-performing, high-engagement organizations that growth and development is a partnership. Employees want to own their development journey, and they want a leader who will be there to help partner with them throughout.

I had the opportunity to go to a conference in 2018. I've gone to many learning conferences over the years, because I was deliberate in working for organizations that believed in investing in my growth in various ways, one of which was attending national conferences. This privilege has taken me to Denver, Orlando, New York, Tampa, San Antonio, Columbus, Nashville, Seattle, Washington, D.C., and the list goes on. The conference in 2018, however, was an eye-opener. It was a smaller conference coordinated by a podcast host, and I quickly noticed something different about it. Most of the people attending were there on their own time and their own dime. They had paid for their travel, their hotel room, and the conference ticket. The conference ticket was about a thousand dollars less than a typical conference ticket, but the experience offered was just as strong, if not stronger. This made the conference both lucrative and affordable for these hungry growth seekers.

As I talked with participant after participant, they shared with me their goals for the conference. They talked about their growth plans. They didn't tell me about what they did for a job; they shared their passions in life and how those connected to their purpose. They shared which speaker they were most excited about and how they planned to invest in themselves in unique ways from the learning at the conference. As we talked and they found out my organization had paid for my trip, each person had the same response, "That's awesome! I wish I worked somewhere that would invest in me that way!"

After the conference ended, I reflected on my experiences and the way each person responded to hearing the difference in how I attended the conference and how they attended. I wondered why these individuals didn't seek out organizations that would invest in them too. Growth and development were clearly a priority for them. They were spending their own money, often coming to this conference in place of going on a vacation somewhere. Many had shared this. It was clear how much development meant to them.

As I reached out and continued to connect with many of these wonderful people after the conference, I started to ask why they were in organizations that didn't invest in them the way mine did. As I talked through each conversation, I found a glaring theme. These individuals actually never talked with their leader about their growth and development because their leader never asked them about it!

I asked them to describe what a typical one-on-one with their leader looked like. Some had no clue what I meant because they never got one-on-one time with their leaders. Others shared that it was one of their least favorite job experiences. Most said one-on-one time was when their leader asked for project updates and then gave them more tasks to complete. If they were given goals, they were organizational goals. Goals that aligned to the top goals in the company. Goals that weren't connected to their purpose, that they had no say in or even fully understood.

As I listened to each share, my heart felt connected through empathy. They wanted to learn, they wanted to be empowered in their development, and they weren't getting those things in their workplaces from their leaders. They didn't complain about this; they just took their development into their own hands. They also didn't realize there were different possibilities and leaders out there who held investing in those they were leading as a top priority and a reason they decided to lead.

This story continues when I wrote my very first article on Peaceful Powered Leadership. By this point, I had been working on this concept with leaders for years but hadn't connected the term to all the associated ideas. This article was going to be the first time Peaceful Powered Leadership was put out into the world in a major online publication. When I submitted the article to one of the company's editors for review, something unique happened. I got back an endearing response. This was unique because when I had heard back from the editors before about articles I had written on other topics, it was only about the context and flow of my writing. Editors would ask questions for clarity or explain they felt the story I shared needed to be firmed up to make my point clearer.

This time the editor mentioned none of these issues. Instead, she shared that the concept of Peaceful Powered Leadership hit home with her and that she wished she could work for a leader one day who lived this way. It was at that moment I knew my passion for this work was truly becoming a calling. A calling to help others because they didn't know what was missing from their workplaces, but when they saw it, it made it easier to describe. It gave them awareness that kind of leadership did exist, and this is how they'd describe it. It made me realize many people wanted this kind of investment from their leaders, and many leaders wanted to provide it, but neither knew how to go about it.

And while with Peaceful Powered Leadership I try to provide a framework for each person's journey in obtaining and providing this support, there are many leaders out there bravely living with a mindset of serving others before self and investing in those they lead. If you are already doing this, great! Let's figure out how you can develop it further. If you aren't investing the way you should in your team yet, that's okay—as long as you've made the decision you are going to start now! If you can't tell yet, this piece of Peaceful Powered Leadership carries heavy weight with me. It connects to my purpose to help others grow and develop and inspire them to take action.

What Investing Shouldn't Look Like

Before we get into how to invest in others, let's make sure you're clear on how *not* to invest in others. I don't typically go down the path of opposites, but I've found this focus on investing in others has become a largely scoped piece over the years, built primarily on opinion, with research and data often left out. Because of these findings, I want to highlight some powerful misconceptions about investing in others so you can self-reflect and hit reset in certain areas if needed.

Venting isn't investing.

I've heard leader after leader share that they grow trust with their team through allowing them to vent. News flash: Allowing venting isn't an investment in others. It's a time waster for all and doesn't actually build trust; it disintegrates it. It promotes a lack of accountability. Let's think about the word venting for a moment. If you look the word up online, there are various definitions. Two of the more common ones focus on providing an outlet or giving free expression. Investment is putting something in. Both of the venting definitions deal with letting something out. Even at its simplest, venting appears to be the opposite of investing.

Some have questioned why venting doesn't build trust. Have you ever stopped and thought about how unhealthy venting is? A common explanation I hear people use when they try to promote venting as a healthy output is: "They needed to get that off their chest. I want them to know I am here for them."

Let's examine this common saying. Did getting it off their chest lead to a solution? I don't know about you, but as a leader, when people have vented to me and I ask them what outcome I can partner with them on to get to a solution, things usually get really quiet. The most common response is, "I just needed to share." Sharing isn't a solution and just because we shared doesn't mean the issue is resolved. People still carry around the emotions associated with this share. It doesn't lead to peace, and it doesn't build trust. Leaders report that they allow venting so that their employees know they can come to them and trust them with this information. I want to challenge this thought process. From my research, here are the three most common venting "shares" to a leader in the workplace:

1. Venting about another team member (and when it isn't venting to the leader, the person is venting about their leader to someone else!)
2. Venting about another team
3. Venting about the organization

As you can see, none of these top three are solution focused. How does venting about another team member grow trust with that team member? How does venting about another team strengthen the relationship with that team? How does venting about the organization lead to stronger engagement in the organization? The answer to all three questions is: It doesn't! When leaders allow people to vent, they are promoting a very unhealthy and unproductive habit. They are also allowing time spent with them to be about this negative type of behavior and conversation instead of conversation that promotes dialogue centered on partnership, growth, and development.

Many times, venting leads to a lack of trust on teams. It provides false, surface-level trust. On the surface, everything seems nice and comfortable, but there are no strong roots of trust below the surface. If you were to dig up the topsoil, the ground below is virtually a sinkhole. People vent to their leader about a team member and get it off their chest, but they get into the habit of not talking with their team member. This promotes unhealthy relationships.

When Jack does something that upsets me, I don't step into courage and talk with Jack about it. Instead, I stay in comfort and I go to my leader and talk with him about it. If you are owning and setting your reality, you will be swimming in accountability and you will start taking venting off the table. Accountable people quickly realize that to stay in ownership of reality, they need to own their next action step. They start to assess their time and are quick to realize venting is a time waster because it doesn't produce action-oriented next steps. It only appears to ease our concerns, but this is short-term and not actually fixing any problems. Stay in ownership and out of venting, and don't deceive yourself into thinking this is a way to invest in others.

Entitlement isn't engagement.

Many leaders I've talked with over the last few years identify employee engagement as a source of sourness rather than peacefulness. They worry about engagement surveys and outcomes affecting their jobs. I've had leader after leader share that their organization has said things like, "If you don't bring your engagement scores up by 10 percent over the next year, there may not be a place here for you as a leader."

First off, if you're leading in an organization that holds engagement survey scores as the primary means to measure engagement, but they don't have research on what is a realistic percentage to expect to move the scores in a one-year period, there are probably some serious engagement violations happening. The scores are probably not going to move because the engagement emphasis isn't on the right thing for the organization. However, if you choose to stay and want to live in peace, know the pieces of engagement that are in your locus of control. Employees have to choose to be engaged. This is a fact. It doesn't matter if you have the best work environment someone could think of producing, if a person decides they don't want to engage in it, they won't. So many leaders focus on making their team happy versus creating an environment around accountability to create engagement partnerships.

Think about a time when you were trying to build employee engagement with someone in the workplace. Often leaders have said, "Tell me how I can help build your engagement." The typical responses include things that will increase perceived happiness. "If you gave us a specialty coffeemaker, then we'll be happy." "If you increased our pay by 5 percent, then we'll be happy." "If you made us a quiet room, then we'll be happy." With each of these examples, all of which I've seen provided by leaders on numerous occasions, the employees' "happiness" lasted about two to six weeks and then they were back asking for the next thing because there was a lack of partnership in finding and exploring the root cause. And when the leader gave the next thing, something other than engagement, by nature of the process, often happened: entitlement!

Because of the approach by the leader, the employees took the approach that this was no longer a partnership, but instead, they were given a door to ask for more. And why wouldn't they? Guess what, the leader led the way for this. From the employees' perspective, their leader was trying to please them. The leader was really trying to engage them, but that isn't often how it is viewed. They asked and they received. If they didn't receive, then they refused. They refused to be engaged. They refused to help out with the new project. They refused to do this and that and the list went on.

Remember this piece of Peaceful Powered Leadership was on investing in others. Please keep in mind that this process looks completely different with highly accountable, highly engaged employees.

Investment is putting something in to help it grow. It is not giving something to someone in order for them to be happy. We want our people to be happy, for sure, but happiness is only a piece of a healthy working environment. Remember this vital truth. If you are more concerned with others liking you than being at peace, peace will not win. Seeking others' approval, especially when accountability isn't associated with it, is far from investing in someone. It usually leads to frustration and being unhappy as we allow the source of our joy to be in someone else's hands.

Growth doesn't come without accountability.

Just like engagement doesn't come without accountability, growth doesn't either. There is a big reason becoming a Peaceful Powered Leader starts with owning our reality. When we have an ownership mindset and carry that mindset with us in word and action, we are being accountable. We must acknowledge this is true for those we are working to invest in as well. One of the most frustrating times in my life, when I was far from peace, was when I tried to invest in someone's growth and development, not realizing the person wasn't actually choosing accountability in the process.

This person would shout from the rooftops about how accountable they were. However, the action didn't always follow. They would share a goal and because I admired the person, I wanted to help them in their growth toward the goal. Sometimes they would actually get upset with me when I would push them in ways they had originally asked for to help with their growth. This was upsetting to me, but because I admired them and wanted to be a part of their journey, I overlooked it as discomfort they may have had in their growth.

As I went on working to help them in their journey, I started to evaluate why I wasn't happy partnering with them. Why was I frustrated with this person but not others I had partnered with? What was different? I wanted to be accountable to the experience and be at peace in the process. As I was going back looking at the person's goals, I realized they weren't actually achieving most of their goals but instead changing direction every four to six months.

They went from one thing to the next in both their physical and mental goals, and each time they did this, I noticed their communication approach would change. It took me a while to catch on, but I realized each time they changed direction and I'd ask about their new goal in order to be of help, some key things occurred. Their tone of voice was very stern. It felt like they were mad I had asked. I would then internalize this and tell myself they were upset with me. As this unhealthy cycle for me continued, I realized I had to be accountable to the situation, change it, and ensure I wasn't storytelling.

As I looked through the goals the person shared with me, they were actually only accomplishing a select few. They were an activities person. They jumped from one activity to the next until discomfort came and then they would move on. They weren't actually growing. They wanted to, that much was clear, but they weren't being accountable to self when the rubber met the road. I tried to talk with the individual about it in different ways, at different times, but the conversation often drifted to a sour place. I eventually removed myself from being a person who invested in them and just happily supported them from the sidelines.

It was a huge weight lifted when I realized my piece had to be owned fully by me and not in the happiness of someone else. I realized that to invest in someone else, they have to be willing to be accountable to themselves. If they are not, it doesn't matter how hard we try, they aren't going to get to their growth goals. We can't do it for them. It moves out of our locus of control and out of our place of peace. Take some time and regularly evaluate your investment in others. Are you investing in counterfeit ways? Is there a lack of happiness in the process for you?

True investment may cause discomfort at times, but the process should still be joyful for you. If it isn't, reflect on why and be accountable to yourself first and foremost in order to get back to peace. Take the actions you need to take even if it means removing yourself from the playing field and sitting on the sidelines. You can still root for the success of the person, but if they aren't accountable and looking for solutions to move from word to action, it will be hard for you to help them and even harder to continue moving forward in peace.

We've explored three specific ways we can make counterfeit investments in others: allowing venting, confusing engagement with entitlement, and continuing to invest when our partner has no accountability. It's important that these be clearly identified. Reflect to ensure you understand them. Take a personal audit to see if you are participating in any of them and think about how you can transition to a more productive approach. This next section will provide a focus on solutions and how Peaceful Powered Leaders invest in others.

What Investing Does Look Like

Investing in others most often means providing our time, which also involves listening to others, energy, and, in some ways, resources. The following are ideas to spark your thought process about investing. Think about these core practices of successful investors and about whether you are currently applying them in your life and how you could open up to investing in others further.

Investors don't get intimidated; they admire.

A major contributor to people's lack of peace is the mindset of comparison. People compare themselves to others in many aspects of their lives, and the workplace is no exception. Peaceful Powered Leaders, however, don't struggle with comparison because they understand their journey is unique. No one else is on it now, nor have they been on it before.

In the age of social media when other people's lives appear to be so much more accessible, it is easy to fall into the path of comparison. However, think about what we do each time we compare ourselves and our lives to others. We expend time, energy, and effort—three resources we could be using in much more productive ways. So often, too, comparison leads to intimidation. When we compare ourselves, we may become intimidated by someone else's success and accomplishments. Judgment of others creeps into our thought process, and the ability to lift up fades as the urge to push away for safety gets stronger.

A much healthier process is to free ourselves from comparison that leads to intimidation by practicing admiration. Peaceful Powered Leaders value others. They admire the true uniqueness others bring forward and seek out ways to help them. These leaders regard others' strengths with admiration and as an opportunity, and they understand each person's journey is different. Sometimes that opportunity is to help continue building someone up through investment in them. Other times, the opportunity is to learn from others through admiration. As a leader, we have the opportunity to help others on their journey.

Many times I've encountered a leader who shared, "I can't afford to lose this person from my team." The Peaceful Powered Leader says instead, "I can't wait to see this person's next step in their career, and I look forward to helping them get there." Because Peaceful Powered Leaders put investment in others at the forefront of their leadership, they have a team of strong individuals who together are powerful. If one moves on in their career, this advance is celebrated, and potential growth opportunities continue to open for other strong team members. The team isn't a weakly built house only standing because of one weight-bearing individual. No, many strong pillars are supporting the house, and it will not topple if one is gone.

Peaceful Powered Leaders want to see their team members move to the next stage in their unique journey. They hire the best talent and best fit for their teams without fear or intimidation that someone may have a stronger skill set than they do in a particular area. They don't shove someone in a corner or at the end of the bench when that team member starts to shine. They help that person shine brighter, because they are confident in both that person's skill set and their own.

Additionally, Peaceful Powered Leaders work to help out other leaders. They don't silo themselves and their teams but instead work to partner with and invest in other leaders and their teams as well. You won't hear a Peaceful Powered Leader tell their team members to hold an idea to their chest and not share it with others. They understand the value of partnership and the ownership that comes with it. If they or their team is struggling to partner with another leader or team, they work to flex their communication style and approach to meet the leader or team where they are. They seek to understand where and why barriers exist, and they think about how and what they can do to take next steps in action to partner with others.

Investors understand there is always a way.

Those who want to grow, want to develop, and want to achieve their goals and dreams are able to do so because they believe there is always a way. Failure is a part of growth, and Peaceful Powered Leaders lead the way with this. They understand the importance of opening the door to creativity and innovation, and with that open door comes experimentation and failure.

They've left the traditional ideals of leadership, ones of telling and directing, in order to invest, open the door to empowerment, and grow. They've already created the environment where accountability thrives, so this approach isn't a free-for-all where an employee doesn't have to own their part in the investment. Peaceful Powered Leaders have ripped off the shame barrier that has been built in so many organizations around failure.

We are human beings, we are imperfect, and we will fail in pursuit of success because that is a part of trying. However, there is always a way to get to where we are aiming for; it just may not be the way we expected. I've had contact with a lot of organizations that claim the mantra, "We are about continuous improvement." Their leaders hide behind this mantra, while at the same time, they direct others how to accomplish the business needs in the organization. They've clearly lost the part of continuous improvement that involves respect for people. If your team isn't bringing forward new ideas and pushing forward toward the success of the team with ownership of business results, it's time to take a step back and do some self-reflection. How have you built an environment that enables investment and empowerment, while helping those you lead be okay with failing? How have you also modeled the mindset that there is always a way?

One of my favorite books, and a big source of learning in my life, is by author Alex Banayan. In his book, *The Third Door*, Banayan shares his five-year journey to interview some of the world's most successful people and gives readers an inside look into how they launched their careers. While Banayan's purpose was to interview and write about these successful people, his story in *The Third Door* became more about him finding a way time and time again to keep his purpose and move his project forward.

From cracking the code to get on *The Price Is Right* to coming up with the right email address to communicate with someone who would eventually become his mentor, Banayan showed that when the front door and the back door to move forward seem to be closed, there is always a third door. With that third door came his powerful revelation that there is always a way if we choose to seek it out. It is an important lesson I have brought into my leadership and the way I invest in others.

My third door in being a stronger Peaceful Powered Leader is vulnerability. I am at peace knowing I don't have all the right questions or answers, and I have no problem sharing that with team members. What I do promise them is that I will partner with them to find a way to help them achieve their goals if they are willing to continue moving forward. We will find a way together.

Over the years, I've encountered leader after leader who has shared with me frustrations about their organization's budget. They report the reason their team's engagement isn't where it needs to be is because funds aren't available to reward and recognize. They've shared that they can't send people to growth opportunities because of the budget. As I listen, I work to withhold judgment, as I don't know the full situation.

When they are finished sharing and ask if I have any advice, I share that I don't. I only have a few questions. I proceed to ask them if they've worked to partner with someone from finance to see what options are available for funding these items within the budget. The answer I most commonly get is, "No." I then ask them if they could try it, and they start sometimes to share why it wouldn't help. Usually by then, they know my reputation of working to own and set reality and be accountable and change their response to, "I suppose I could."

From there, I ask them what solutions they would bring forward if finance said, "Yes, we'd be happy to partner and look for a way." Most of the time, they share honestly that they haven't thought about this and need to prepare for that option. Sometimes they have some ideas they share.

I then ask, "Can I see those ideas in written form?" Less than 5 percent have been able to share in written form. The last question I ask is, "What would it take for you to get a plan on paper or in a document with multiple solutions [I am direct in using "multiple" because only bringing one solution forward isn't actually bringing solutions. It is bringing your desired want] to share with finance?" I ask this question because from my experience, and from what leaders I've worked with have shared, they've had fewer rejections when someone sees they have put pen to paper for a well-laid-out plan.

I share this line of questioning, because so often we (myself included) go to the easy answer of door one or door two. Door three is rarely easy, rarely clear-cut, and often rarely used, so we don't know what is on the other side and that can be scary. When we are investing in those we are leading, though, we should be working to find a way. In our efforts to do this, we are teaching them the process as well.

Investors treat each connection as a potential people powered moment.

At the beginning of 2017, I began work on a book that would eventually be titled *People Powered Moments*. As I was writing this part memoir, part lessons-to-live-by book, I realized how much of my life had been impacted by both large and small deliberate moments of connection with others. That includes people who took time to make a connection through their investment in me and me focusing on the opportunity to do the same with others.

People have always been a priority to me, and I love listening to people. I once had a friend say to me, "You genuinely care what other people are saying and that is rare." Her statement took me by surprise because I honestly felt that was the norm for people. The more research I did, though, the more I found that many people took part in a conversation to simply wait for someone else to listen to what they had to say. This approach misses out on so many rewarding aspects of truly connecting to others.

One of the biggest barriers I've faced in life is "small talk." I don't do it well because I don't want to discuss the weather. I want you to know that I want to know about you. What is important in your life? Why do you do what you do? I've become used to getting surprised stares when fifteen minutes into a conversation with someone new I'm asking them about what goals they are striving for and how I can help. The surprised stare, many have shared with me, is because they can tell that I genuinely want to know and that I sincerely want to help, and they haven't had someone ask them those types of questions before. It is true; I genuinely want to help.

I've had an initial conversation with someone, not spoken to them again for months or sometimes even years, and have had them reach out through social media to ask to talk again. This has happened multiple times and the talk is always about helping them by investing in a coaching conversation with them. I share this because I've found that living a life with the intent to truly connect with others leads to some awesome moments, both for those I'm connecting with and myself.

When you focus on others with the mindset of "How can I help?" it opens the door for some powerful connections.

Two moments of initial connection and investment in March of 2019 led to important and surprising results for me. On March 7, preparing to speak at a state conference in Washington, I was going through the event app on my phone, inviting people to my breakout session. If I knew the company a conference attendee worked for, I'd connect to them with something about their company, usually because I was excited to hear about their experiences with the organization. I came across a person who worked for a particular company, a company most well-known for creating small collectable figures of pop culture characters from television, film, video games, etc. My son loved the company and had a collection of the figures. The person was a Human Resources team member, so I shared about my breakout, as well as how my son was a huge fan of the company. I didn't hear back from the person that evening.

On the morning of March 8, as I was preparing for the conference, I noticed I had a missed call from my wife's phone. It was around the time my son usually got up for school, and because I traveled often, we had a routine of my wife calling to let my son say good morning when he woke up. We usually talked for a few minutes before we all launched into school and work for the day. I called my wife back and when she answered the phone, I couldn't understand what she was saying—she was sobbing and screaming.

I asked her to slow down and told her I couldn't understand her. She slowed down enough for me to make out that she was saying our son was having a seizure and was completely unresponsive. This had never happened before. I asked her a few questions and then told her she needed to call 9-1-1 immediately. I was so upset that I wasn't home to be there to help my son and support my wife in this moment. I was instead almost six hours away. I thought positively though and told myself that paramedics would be able to help and my son would be okay.

About five minutes passed before I got a call from a paramedic. He didn't know my wife and I had talked, and his call was one of the most terrifying moments of my life. I answered the phone, and the man on the other line asked if I was Cayden Narlock's father. I said I was, and he informed me he was with the paramedics. He proceeded to say, "I'm sorry to have to make this call Mr. Narlock and share this news with you." My mind immediately went to a tough place. The only time I've heard those words with that tone was when people shared that someone had passed away.

Time froze ever so briefly for me, and I can remember exactly where I was standing in the hotel room and what I was looking at. He then continued, "Your son has had a seizure and paramedics are on the way to help him. Your wife called us and asked that we contact you."

Time sped up again. I told the man my wife and I had talked and I was the one that told her she needed to call the paramedics. The man said, "Oh good, we were unaware and wanted to help your wife out." We talked for a minute longer as I asked a few questions.

Ten minutes later, my wife called to tell me that our son hadn't stopped seizing and they were trying to get him stable enough to put him in the ambulance and take him to the hospital. I was struggling. I immediately started pacing, thinking through options to help. We had been in Bend, Oregon for less than a year and only knew one family we were both close with. I called them and, without hesitation, they headed to the hospital to be there for my wife and son. I still was thinking that once my son got to the hospital, he'd be stabilized and be home soon. This, unfortunately, wasn't the case. His body kept seizing.

After about two hours at the hospital, they got Cayden's body to essentially shut down through medication and intubating him. The doctors couldn't say if the seizing had actually stopped, but he was now stable. My wife explained all this when she called to let me know the decision had been made to fly Cayden to a children's hospital with a pediatric neurologist in Portland, Oregon. It was at this point that the severity of the situation hit me. I told my wife I was getting in the car to come home. She said that didn't make sense because they could be in Portland well before I got back home.

I stood in the room, feeling helpless as my wife told me to go facilitate the learning discussion I was leading that morning. She said it was a waiting time for now. She was very strong for me, but I found out later from our friends that when off the phone, my wife was struggling greatly. Our friend, Zach, stayed by our son's bedside as his wife, Nicole, took my wife home to pack a bag for us in preparation to go to Portland. She also helped clean my son's mattress. It was early morning when the seizure happened, and a side effect was he urinated all over it. He never wet the bed, so that was not a normal experience for us. They cleaned off the sheets and mattress and grabbed the bag.

I facilitated that morning and, looking back, should not have done so. I notified the event organizer of what was occurring, and he urged me to leave. I knew about fifty to seventy-five people were coming to my breakout session, and I didn't want to let them down. He shared with me that they would understand, but in my mind, there wasn't anything else to do. I knew I'd still make it to Portland before my wife and son, facilitating or not, so I stayed. Twenty minutes into the discussion just around the point of discussing owning your outcomes as a leader, I shared what was occurring in my life. I am a very transparent speaker. I storytell and share vulnerable moments at times, but I knew as I was sharing this, I shouldn't have been up front facilitating.

This was different. I didn't feel fully in control of what I was saying, even though I was trying so hard to be. I shared that I didn't believe in bad days. As an owner of my life, I only believed in bad moments in our days. I shared that I was having a good moment being with the group but had a very bad moment learning about my son two hours prior to speaking with them. I could see shock on some of their faces. I finished the talk. I don't remember a lot of it, but I know I wasn't sharp or crisp in my delivery like I normally am. My timing was off, and I was all over the place on my points. It was a great lesson learned. What I didn't know, though, was that an attendee from the collectible company was in the group. My story will come back around to that people powered moment shortly.

I finished the event and the organizer gave me a hug and said to call if I needed absolutely anything. He was an amazing individual named Andrew. I got in my car and started making my way through Seattle downtown traffic to make the two-and-a-half-hour drive to Portland. I did make it to the hospital before my wife and son, who were still in route when I arrived. I was relieved when I saw my wife and shocked when I saw my son. He was lying motionless. A breathing tube was in his mouth and, at that point, we hadn't heard his voice in about eighteen hours. At this point, you might be asking yourself, where is the promised people powered moment about focusing on investing with others? It is coming.

As my wife and I embraced, she shared with me that Zach and Nicole were on their way to the hospital. I was shocked. Yes, I had asked them to be there for my wife when I couldn't be, but there was no reason for them to travel three hours to Portland for us. That is who they are, though. They are amazing human beings and guess how I met them? Through investing in Nicole.

Nicole was a new team member of mine in 2011. I was the corporate trainer and educational coordinator for a group of trainers. Nicole was hired as one of the training specialists. She was eager to learn and was an amazing strategist. I was excited to work with her and, little did I know, she and her husband would be playing such a significant role in my family's life eight years later.

When I met Nicole, I had been formally teaching and training for six years, and I partnered with her to help her grow by sharing my knowledge, failures, and findings over those years. She was open to learning about facilitating and training, and I was open to learning about strategy and communication. We invested in each other in unique ways the whole time we worked together. We actually only worked together for a short time but continued to connect and grow as friends and our families did too. In 2018, when my family and I were deciding our next move and career steps, Nicole opened the door for me to work with her as an internal coach on the team she was building in an organization with wonderful leaders who were jumping at the opportunity to grow and develop. And now, she and her husband were right there beside us as we experienced one of the toughest moments in our family's history. They were an incredible support and I can't thank them enough. One people powered moment of investment with Nicole in 2011 led to a long-time connection that has brought so much joy to my family's life.

At about 2:00 a.m. on March 9, 2019, we heard our son's voice for the first time in over twenty-four hours. It was such a relief. He was diagnosed with focal point epilepsy, and we were told that he should grow out of it between the ages of twelve and fifteen. We were so happy to hear this, and he's been doing great.

Now, I'll circle back to pick up that promised people powered moment. About a week after Cayden was discharged from the hospital, my wife and I debated on following through on taking him to a comic convention in Seattle as we had promised. He didn't remember any of his time in the hospital, was still recovering from what his body went through, but he was begging us to go. We wanted to keep as much normalcy as possible in his life since we had already been notified by his school of some of the things he could no longer do because of his epilepsy.

The deciding factor, though, was a special offer: an invitation for Cayden to tour the collectible company's headquarters. We knew he would absolutely freak out if he could do this, and the headquarters were about forty minutes outside of Seattle. The person from the company who made this generous offer wasn't in my breakout session at the Seattle conference, but her team member was, and she'd heard what happened to our son. This wonderful person was the woman from Human Resources who I had only briefly connected with through the event social media app. I was astonished by her extending this heartfelt offer at a very hard time for our family.

We kept the tour a surprise for Cayden, who was truly amazed and exceedingly excited when we pulled up to the headquarters. We got to use the special employee entrance, and as we went from one area to the next on the tour, the smile on his face that we hadn't seen much of since he left the hospital was out in full force. The human resources representative and I talked while my son and wife went around taking pictures, and she informed me Cayden would also be treated to a shopping spree. I was so touched and grateful for this people powered experience. When I asked her how we could thank her, she said the smile on Cayden's face was enough. I then thought to myself, "Jared, what can you give that is special back to this wonderful person?" Then it hit me—invest in her. I shared with her that I was a certified coach and I would love to partner with her on her journey. I gave her my information, and she thankfully took me up on my offer. It has been such a joy interacting with her.

I share these two intersecting stories because they both demonstrate how awesome human beings can be and how the simple act of connecting, and, from there, investing, can bring unexpected wonders into your life. I don't ever invest in someone expecting a return for me but instead a return for them in their growth and development on their journey. Seeing them succeed in achieving their goals and dreams is my return. In these two instances, however, there was even more of a return than that.

You never know what will happen when you choose to invest in others. When your life is focused on contributing to others instead of looking for what you can get out of them, amazing doors open and wonderful experiences arise. It is a peaceful place to venture through. How are you connecting with others today? Do you have a focus on investing in others for their growth and development? Take some time to go through the connection exercise below to do an inventory on where your connection points currently are and how you can build upon them.

Making Connections that Matter Exercise

You may have noticed most of the exercises in this book involve questions. Questions lead us to think, and thinking often leads us to self-reflection. As a coach, the primary way I help others is through listening to them and asking them questions. They find the answers and work to identify and take the next actionable steps. I work to get them to a different place of reflection they may not have been before. Sometimes they are too close to a situation to see something, and as they share, I ask questions. Sometimes they share that they've asked themselves that question before. Many times, though, they share that they hadn't thought about that question, and it leads to a different thought process or helps build further on an idea.

I share the purpose of my method to provide insight into why you'll continue to find a lot of questions in this book. We are all different. As you read this book, you are on a different journey than someone else reading this book. If I were to tell you to "do this technique" or "try this out," my recommendation may be completely irrelevant for you because it doesn't connect with you. A question, though, allows for a third door to open that is unique to each person. This journey is yours. No one is checking up on you. Don't be fearful of judgment as you answer but be open to growth and exploration.

For this exercise, take time to think about and write down answers to each question. Then reflect on how you answered. Are you where you want to be, or are there aspects of your current approach to connecting and investing you'd like to change? How can you take active steps to make those changes? What are the discoveries or learnings you've already experienced in your journey with this book that can contribute to next steps?

1. **How do you work to connect with people currently?**
2. Reflection: What do you like about your answer? What are pieces you would like to add to, change, or keep in your current approach?

3. **How do you scope and define your purpose for connecting with someone?**

4. Reflection: Are you seeking mutual benefit and value in the relationship? Do you think about how you can invest in that person?

5. **Do you seek out people who have similar values?**

6. Reflection: Are you aware of the vital friends you have in your life? Are there any vital friends you would like in your life that you don't have?

A sidenote to this question is the term vital friends. I borrow it from Tom Rath, author of *Vital Friends: The People You Can't Afford to Live Without*. The book was life-changing for me. It helped me identify and understand many of the connections I had in my life. It also helped me understand how I was expecting others to invest in me and why I struggled when they didn't meet my expectations.

I realized my wife wasn't, and probably shouldn't be, the only vital friend I needed, and this was okay. Sharing this new insight with her helped grow and improve our relationship immensely. I also realized there was a key vital friend I had been searching for and didn't find in my current connections. I had animosity toward many friends because they weren't able to connect with me in a particular way. After taking active steps toward growth with the learnings from Rath's book, I realized it was okay that these people didn't serve a particular role, and I became more peaceful when I could easily identify what I was looking for or needed at a particular time in my growth and the person or people I was going to work to partner with. I had a different outlook and intent for connection that truly wasn't intended to be self-serving or hold expectations. It was coming from a place of connection, growth, and investment intended for all parties involved.

1. **How do you open the door to investing in others?**

2. Reflection: Do those you lead share the ways they would like you to invest in them? If not, how can you open the door to these discussions?
3. **How do you celebrate with your connections?**
4. Reflection: When someone you've invested in hits a milestone, whether small or large, how do you celebrate for them or with them?

Leaders have great intentions about investing. Oftentimes, though, without deliberate focus, investment lies on the back burner and surfaces only when a reminder is put in front of us. Just like with gratitude, take time to make the process of investment a habit that doesn't need a reminder.

How'd you answer the question on celebrating with your connections? I can tell you I haven't always been the best connector or celebrator. I tended to connect in ways that were comfortable to me with people who communicated similarly to me. Meanwhile amazing people would be standing in front of me, asking to connect, asking to celebrate. As a leader, I realized the importance of flexing my communication style to connect and celebrate. When I started to do this, true investment was happening all around. It took work on my part but work I was thankful to be doing. It powered my peace in a unique and more meaningful way.

As I worked on steps for becoming a Peaceful Powered Leader, I struggled with ordering them—what should come before or after what—especially where to place investing in others and setting sacred time with ourselves. At times, I felt that Peaceful Powered Leaders needed to first understand how to set sacred time with themselves to truly be able to properly and peacefully invest in others. I realized through my experiences, though, that while leaders tend to struggle at times with both pieces of the process, they were often more open to discussing investing in others. Only after that discussion were they more excited about exploring setting sacred time with themselves. I believe they felt less selfish about the topic and understood how the two truly go hand in hand. And with that shared, let's venture into the next piece of becoming a Peaceful Powered Leader: setting sacred time with yourself.

Thought Leader Perspective – Kristen Hadeed

Kristen Hadeed is the founder of Student Maid and author of Permission to Screw Up: How I Learned to Lead by Doing (Almost) Everything Wrong. *To learn more, checkout LinkedIn: Kristen Hadeed; IG: @kristenhadeed.*

Narlock: Student Maid is known for many great things and one is having employees who feel empowered. How did you build an environment that creates this feeling and how does your team help ensure new employees feel it from the start of their employment?

Hadeed: It starts with our core values. I was really inspired by the founder of Zappos, Tony Hsieh, when I started Student Maid, and he created core values for his company by asking for suggestions from his team. So I did the same thing. From all the suggestions I got, my team and I narrowed it down to the ten we felt not only were the most important but that also captured the culture at Student Maid. The values became our guide for decision-making.

For decisions big and small, we use our values to help us choose the best course of action. And that works on an individual level too. Part of empowering our team members means putting the power to make decisions in their hands, but it's hard to do that if you don't have guidelines. So we tell our team members that as long as the decisions they make on the job are in line with our ten values, we will not fault them, even if the outcome of their choice isn't ideal. We'll know that they had the company's best interests at heart.

Over the years, we've put other systems in place to preserve our culture of empowerment and autonomy. We call our employee handbook *The Guidebook* because it focuses more on what our team members are allowed to do than what they aren't. In *The Guidebook*, we talk about the concept of "the line," which is our way of explaining the relationship between our leadership team and our team members. Basically, it's a two-sided system: In order for Student Maid to work, both our leadership team and our team members need to be willing to show up and "stand at the line" every day. Standing at the line for team members means they're choosing to invest in themselves by learning from their mistakes; they're communicating openly and fully, especially when there's a problem; and they take their work responsibilities seriously. And the leadership team stands at the line by investing in our team members' growth; coaching and guiding them as they learn from their mistakes; and continuing to provide a nurturing, supportive work environment.

We introduce the core values, *The Guidebook*, and the concept of the line during the first few days of training so our new hires are on board from the start. We want them to understand that whether they've been with us for two days or two years, we trust them. There's no "trial period" for empowerment; we empower them to try from day one.

Narlock: In your book, *Permission to Screw Up: How I Learned to Lead by Doing (Almost) Everything Wrong*, you do a wonderful job of sharing with the reader the experience of failure and perseverance that leads to succeeding through trying. How do you help your team understand failure is okay in your company and the connection it has to success?

Hadeed: The biggest thing we do is to lead by example (and by "we," I mean our leadership team). We strive to be as transparent as possible with our team, so that means that when we make mistakes—especially ones that impact them or the company—we own up to them. And we make sure to pair this transparency with accountability.

It's okay to make mistakes, but it's not okay to make mistakes without learning from them. We hold each other accountable to learning and growing and making sure our mistakes teach us something. It's only failure when you're not invested in doing things differently the next time around to try to produce a better result. That's how we connect it to success: If your mistakes help you learn or give you a new perspective, that's a win in our book.

Narlock: Have you ever made a self-serving or self-preserving decision in lieu of making a decision that served the better interest of those you were leading? If so, can you share the story and what you learned from the experience?

Hadeed: Our busiest time of year is called move-out season. It's a three-week period at the end of the summer where thousands of student apartments need to be cleaned at the same time. Apartment complexes issue contracts to cleaning companies and other vendors to handle some or all of their units, and if you can hire a team big enough, you can make really good money in a short amount of time.

I started participating in move-out season with my team the same year I started Student Maid. Every year after that, I would hire a bigger and bigger team until we were hiring hundreds of people every summer. (Our regular year-round team consisted of about seventy-five people at most, so this was a huge undertaking.) I would sign contracts with dozens of properties all around town, and even though the work was physically exhausting and, frankly, miserable at times (we're talking about cleaning filthy apartments in the summertime in Florida), somehow, we always came through for our clients and cleaned every single unit we were contracted to clean on time.

But hitting those goals came at a big price. The contracts gave us so much money and a higher profit margin than any other work our company did the rest of the year, but the clients we worked with during move-out season weren't treating our people—or our company—well. First, we had to agree to their pricing, which was ridiculously low. The only way to make any money at all was to clean a huge number of units. And on top of that, property managers would make outrageous demands that sometimes had our teams cleaning through the night to try to meet them.

It was no surprise to me when some of the people we would traditionally ask to help manage our team in the summertime started to plan vacations during move-out season just so they wouldn't have to be there! I didn't blame them; I didn't want to be there either. But year after year, I put us through it, even though I knew I was making our team miserable. I did it for a couple reasons: 1) I'd worked so hard to build these relationships with local property managers, and I didn't want to end them and potentially cut us off from a huge amount of revenue, and 2) I was afraid of what people would say if we downsized. In business, we talk about how downsizing equals failing. I knew that if we no longer signed these contracts to clean thousands of units, we would no longer need to hire hundreds of team members, and people around town would look at that and think we must be doing something wrong. I kept us in that place because I was so afraid of what everyone else would think if we stopped doing that kind of work.

Years later, we finally had a serious discussion as a company about dropping move-out season altogether. And surprisingly, what we decided was that we didn't want to completely stop doing it. No matter how miserable move-out season made us, good things always came from it: It gave team members a chance to step up and be leaders; it brought our team together to work toward a common goal like nothing else did; and, at the end of the day, it gave us a much-needed revenue boost. But we also knew that we couldn't continue to do move-out season the way we had always done it.

So we came up with a solution: We would figure out how to do move-out season on our terms. We would work only with people who share our values and who we knew would treat our people well. We drew up our own contract with our own pricing and terms that ensured we would never work too hard for too little return. And instead of hiring hundreds of people, we would hire only a couple dozen and focus on giving them a great experience and introduction to our company. We had no idea if any property would even sign our contract, and if no one did, then that would be the end of it; we wouldn't do it unless we could do it our way. But it worked.

We now work with a handful of properties that give us all or most of their units and pay our pricing, which helps us bring in a comparable amount of revenue to years past. Our culture is night-and-day different; though the work is still exhausting and we still have to pull late nights, our smaller team is so much more tight-knit and willing to come through for each other. We used to have people quit right and left after just a couple days on the job, but now, a majority of the people we hire for move-out season see it through to the end.

The biggest thing I've learned from this is that giving up on something, even if it's really hard or it seems like a bad situation, isn't always the only or the best option. It's worth it to look at the full picture, all the pros and cons, and see if there's a way you can make it work for you, especially if the situation has some upsides, like move-out season did.

Narlock: What three things bring you the most joy as a leader?

Hadeed: #1: Development Day. Development Day is the only time everyone in our company is in the same room at the same time, and it happens just once a quarter. Part of it is reserved for company updates and getting feedback on new projects and systems, but the biggest part—the part I'm in charge of—is for personal development. I'm so removed from the day-to-day that I don't get to see our students that much, so it's the one time I get to be with everyone. The focus of Development Day is learning and growing, which is the thing I'm most passionate about. I love that I get to teach, I get to see how much our students are growing, and I get to help them grow even more.

#2: Leadership team workshops. Once a month, our leadership team, which consists of me and three other women, gets together for a full day (or two) workshop. Part of it is dedicated to taking care of ourselves personally, working on our relationships, and growing as people, and part of it is dedicated to taking care of the business and working through tough obstacles. The workshops bring me joy because we're a remote team, so it's the one time a month when we all get to be together uninterrupted. We get to work through really hard things and grow together in powerful ways and have conversations that challenge us. I always leave these workshops feeling closer and more connected to my team and just so grateful that we all get to work together.

#3: Alumni. Nothing brings a smile to my face faster than when I see a Student Maid alum thriving. I get really happy when I see people who have worked at Student Maid take what they learned from us and use it in their own lives and careers. A great example of this is a former Student Maider named Danny. Danny started a weight-loss clinic, and he decided to create core values for it based on Student Maid's core values. The result was that nurses he hired said they preferred working at his clinic more than others nearby. They loved that they had ownership of their jobs and that they could come to him if they ever had problems or suggestions.

I help other businesses, too, and while it's great to see how they use what I teach them, it's so amazing when I get to see our Student Maid team members taking what we taught them to heart and using it for good in the world.

Narlock: If you had only one story to share as your legacy as a leader, what would it be?

Hadeed: I would tell the infamous story of my HR intern, Lizzie, and her $40,000 mistake. Here's how it goes:

Shortly after I started the company, I met Lizzie at a career fair. She was studying abroad from the UK and wanted to learn everything she could about business during her time at the University of Florida. I hired her on the spot. She picked up everything I taught her pretty quickly: She helped me conduct interviews, created the first version of our employee handbook, and all kinds of other HR-related things.

After a few months, I decided to give Lizzie an enormous responsibility: I put her in charge of payroll. I thought it'd look great on her resume because not many interns get to say they did payroll for an entire company. But, obviously, payroll is a huge deal, and it's one of those things you just can't mess up. When our payroll company found out I was handing over the task to Lizzie, they cautioned me that it wasn't a good choice and said I should give it to someone with more experience. I didn't listen to them, though. I believed in Lizzie and knew she could do it. I walked her through the process a couple times and then handed her the reins.

Long story short, Lizzie messed up big time. The first time she submitted payroll on her own, she mistakenly overpaid twenty-seven people by $40,000. So instead of paying people $200, for example, Lizzie paid them for 200 *hours*. Yikes. (Our bank account definitely didn't have room for an error that big.)

When I discovered what had happened, I called Lizzie immediately. I didn't yell and scream and blame her for screwing up (though, of course, a small part of me wanted to). Instead, I asked if she had any ideas about what we should do to fix the problem. After a few minutes, she came up with a pretty good solution: We should get in touch with each of the twenty-seven people, tell them what happened and ask (more like beg) them not to spend the extra money. Then, she would call our payroll company and see if they could reverse the transaction. I followed her lead, and several nerve-wracking days later (it felt like years), every cent of that $40,000 was returned to our account.

Two weeks later, when it was time to submit payroll again, I asked Lizzie to do it. She was shocked that I still wanted her in charge of payroll, but I saw how well she'd handled the problem, and I wanted to give her a chance to prove to herself that she was capable of doing better. And you know what? She did. Lizzie never made a payroll error again.

Lizzie's mistake was a lesson for both of us. It helped me realize that I never wanted anyone at our company to be afraid of failing. I wanted them to see that messing up is an important part of growth as long as we learn from it and do better the next time. I wanted to make Student Maid a place where people felt safe screwing up so they could become more confident in their abilities and be more successful as a result of their time with us.

As for Lizzie, she told me that in every job interview she's had since her internship with us, she's told this infamous payroll story. Instead of focusing on the fact that she messed up, her potential employers were impressed that she took action to handle her mistake. Today, she works at a company in the UK, and because of her experience at Student Maid, she trusts the people on her team with big responsibilities and teaches them not to fear their screwups but to grow from them.

That's the goal. We trust people with responsibilities they might not be ready for, and when they mess up, we hold them accountable to figuring out a solution on their own. And then we trust them with that thing again, and when they do it right that time, they learn that they're capable and they can trust themselves to handle big, tough things and grow from their mistakes.

There are so many more stories like Lizzie's, but the legacy is that we help people understand that they're capable and give them the room to see what they're made of. We support them in a challenging, but loving, way that helps them figure out how they're going to make their mark on the world.

Chapter 5
Peaceful Powered Leaders Set Sacred Time with Themselves

"That sure would be nice." This five-word sentence is the most common response I've received over the years when I discuss making time to focus on growth and development and reflecting on how people invest in themselves. I remember vividly one day working with a group of executive leaders who worked for a nonprofit organization. The title of my talk was "Ownership Is Leadership: How We Can Own Our Business." This talk is intended for leaders who don't own their own business but instead work for a company and are leaders in that company. It ties back to Chapter 1 and owning our reality. As I spoke with leaders that day, I shared that time for weekly reflection was vital for anyone, and especially those leading teams. We should be making sacred time for ourselves. Right after saying this, one executive looked up and awkwardly laughed and said, "That sure would be nice." The leader proceeded to tell me how busy he was and why sacred time wasn't attainable for him.

I told him it was attainable if he decided he wanted to put in the time and discipline to make it happen. He proceeded to tell me I didn't understand the pressures of being in the C-suite. I shared with him that generalizing will almost always keep us from the forward progression we want in our lives. I shared that only he knew his reality, and he was right. I didn't know it, nor did I know it for anyone else in the room except myself.

He didn't know the reality of the other executives sitting in the room with him. He knew pieces of their reality but not the full picture. He knew generalizations about other executive teams, but not their full reality. I started to name executive leaders from well-known companies who had shared how they invested in themselves through the discipline of sacred time.

I let him know I wasn't there to debate with him but to help if he chose to let me. He thankfully did, and over the next year, there was a huge shift in the type of leader he was. He realized each step was a choice and that included the steps in our mind. If we say we don't have time for sacred time with ourselves, we will make the choice to not have time. Spending time with ourselves, however, is such a peaceful activity, and it is essential to becoming a Peaceful Powered Leader. We must discipline ourselves to take time to slow down. We are in a fast-moving world where technology has triggered us to a new type of progression.

Slowing down doesn't always refer to pace. Slowing down might be taking fifteen minutes a day for self-reflection. Slowing down might be going outside and playing ball with our children and being fully present in the moment. Slowing down may be cooking at home while listening to music or a podcast and really just listening in those moments. Sacred time is a must and it is different for everyone. However, it should include these three disciplines:

1. Detachment and reflection
2. Growth, including strategy
3. Investment, instead of spending

Let's spend some time exploring what each of these involves and why and how you might incorporate them in your sacred time.

Sacred Time Discipline #1 – Detachment and Reflection

Each Friday night when my family goes to sleep or Saturday morning before they wake up, I have one of my focused detachment and reflection sessions. I love them! They are an essential part of my week. I go downstairs in our home and I sit down in my brown recliner. I have nothing with me except my journal and a pen. I start to go through the following questions (yes, questions again!):

- What went well in the week?
- Are there areas where I didn't try my best and want to in the future?
- What are the areas I would've liked to address or approached in a different manner?
- What did I learn in the week?
- How will I apply the learnings and put them into growth actions?
- Are there moments I would've changed? Why?
- What is on the horizon for the next week and month?
- How do the decisions I make in the coming week affect the following week, month, and year?
- How am I going to celebrate this week?
- Is there anyone I need to prepare to celebrate with this week?
- Am I focusing on all aspects of my life the way I want to? (This includes family, friends, development, growth, career, travel, hobbies, etc.)
- What did I learn from my discomfort or failings this week?
- What did I learn from my successes?

This list of questions can be extended, but this is a great starting point and are the questions that yield insights for me. Before reading further, try this exercise. Put the book down after you finish this paragraph. Get a piece of paper or a journal, if you have one, and start answering these questions. Take the time to write each question out and the accompanying answer. Free yourself of distractions. Put the phone away. Close the laptop. Turn the television off. Whatever you need to do to detach and start reflecting on the questions. Your answers don't have to be extraordinary. Just write, be honest with yourself, and at the end, write down how you feel about the experience after finishing.

I hope you chose to do the exercise and aren't reading this sentence before doing so!

If you are like me and so many others I have worked with, you found the exercise surprisingly freeing and are excited about some of your responses. It may have been especially exciting and novel to answer the first question: What went well this week? What's the significance of this question? Focusing on what went well isn't a natural habit for most people. Instead, people go to the other end of the line and give priority to what didn't go well.

As we take the opportunity to focus on what went well, it puts us in a different mindset. It is a mindset of celebration, appreciation, and accomplishment. It involves an answer that typically came about because solutions were put into place and action was taken. It focuses on the *can* instead of *can't* and has the ability to lead us to productive next steps. Think about your mood as you went through this exercise and answered this question and the others. If you were free of distraction, what other items came to mind as you reflected on the questions provided?

I learned early on in my leadership journey how powerful reflection could be. As I started to research the topic, I came across study after study that solidified this belief. One of the strongest corroborations came from Jennifer Porter, an executive coach who describes the most useful reflection as reflection that "involves the conscious consideration and analysis of beliefs and actions for the purpose of learning."[7] Porter also shared that the hardest clients she works with are "those who won't reflect—particularly leaders who won't reflect on *themselves.*"[8]

Have you ever been around a person who appears to be flying by the seat of their pants? This, unfortunately, is how many employees see their leaders. They watch them jump from meeting to meeting and go week to week, not providing a vision or strategy, but simply working to put one fire out and move to the next. These leaders shoot from the hip when providing ideas and next steps, relying on previous knowledge and experience. Detachment and self-reflection offer two essentials for leaders: peace and growth. When we have sacred time set aside that we discipline ourselves to hold to, we can move away from frantic reaction and enjoy a peaceful time where our mind is purposefully creating a path to healthy action.

How can you work to build in time for detachment and reflection into your weekly routine? Start thinking about this and, rest assured, I have an exercise coming up that can help!

Sacred Time Discipline #2 – Growth, Including Strategy

Not only does detachment and self-reflection allow for assessment of our current state, but it also opens the door for forward movement, for next steps to growth. Investing in ourselves should be a must for us. Over the years, I've regularly asked leadership groups this question: Did you spend as much time this month on your growth as you did reviewing the budget you are accountable for? Less than 5 percent of leaders I've worked with answer with a yes. Most leaders openly admit that growth is at the bottom of priorities for them. They don't get asked about their growth by their leader, but they do get asked about their department's financials. Just because no one asks about it doesn't mean it shouldn't be a priority. If you haven't intentionally focused on your own growth before, it can seem like a daunting process to start. It can even, initially, be an uncomfortable process. This is normal. Growth often causes discomfort as we push ourselves beyond our current limits. As you start new growth and self-investment processes, I want you to think about it like a new workout routine.

Workout programs typically are scheduled out for ninety days. Let's examine why this is and why it works so well for those who follow through for ninety days. There is a common misconception that twenty-one days builds a new habit. This may be true for small habits but not for lifestyle changes. A lifestyle change takes approximately sixty days. I've interacted with many people who have stopped these ninety-day workout programs in the first thirty days. When they explain why, they share that between days twenty and thirty, they are sore, they are not seeing the changes in their body or weight they envisioned, and they decide it isn't worth it. I feel so empathetic when I hear this because these individuals didn't realize they were so close to seeing the change they worked so hard for over those twenty to thirty days. In fact, they were over halfway there.

Typically, it is around day forty-five that people start to see the changes in their body, and the workout process starts to feel more like a habit than a grueling new routine. The tipping point starts to occur. The workouts don't cause the soreness or discomfort like they did the first few weeks. The motions start to feel more normal, and people start to see a visible difference in themselves. The drive and motivation push forward because the benefits are now clearly evident. The same is true for real growth in ourselves.

We should be spending sacred time with our development writing out our ninety-day plan. Where do we want to go? How do we want to push ourselves? What does discomfort look like around the goal? What are the pieces we are nervous about? Call them out and think through how you will overcome them when they come forward. This is a huge piece of strategy.

People who invest in themselves and their growth usually have a great strategy. They start with the end in mind. Are you going to be able to accomplish this goal alone? This question is vital when it comes to development. People are willing to invest money when a return is chancy, like in stocks. This isn't the case when you invest in yourself. You are investing in something that gives you a return for the rest of your life. This is why it baffles me when people don't want to spend the money on working with a coach or going to a learning conference.

Just like you spend the money on a personal trainer, or a workout video program, you should be spending money on a development coach if you know you need some help along the path to your goals. Similar to the process of working out in a way that truly pushes your limits, a development coach can push you to new types of questioning that allow you to explore new development methods and paths of thinking.

I am a certified coach and also have and continue to work with coaches in my development. I once heard a person say to their friend: "Why would you work with him? He just shared with you he has his own coach. If he was that good, why would he need a coach?" We had a great discussion on this topic after that statement. I have had different coaches over the years and that is because I've evolved and developed. I've taken strategy thinking to new heights, partly because of different coaches and the way they provided new lines of questioning, exposure to new tools I wasn't aware of, and the list goes on. These individuals helped me grow, just like professional bodybuilders have coaches who help them with their poses, and those coaches know their limits. When their client has outgrown them, they let the client know and usually have a reference ready to give them.

The same is true around our mental mindset building. These people, these coaches, see us in a new and different light. They can't do the work for us, but they can plant seeds that help us grow and branch in new directions. This is part of strategy of how we develop. Beyond the benefits of having a coach as part of your investment in yourself, let's explore the benefits of focusing on your growth and development.

Benefit 1 - It is self-exploration.

When we spend time actively and intently focusing on our growth and development, we are getting to know ourselves in new ways. We explore our limiting beliefs and work to break through them. We explore our pressure points and what really makes us uncomfortable. We develop plans to push through the discomfort, often reaching places that we didn't know we could get to. We start to see who we can become instead of remaining stuck with a person we put limits around because we weren't actually taking the sacred time to develop.

Benefit 2 – It gives us a stronger connection to our purpose.

My purpose in life is to help others grow and develop and inspire others to take action in their lives. I struggled to find this, but as I worked on my own development, my purpose or why in life became so much more vivid. This has happened with so many of my coaching clients too. I remember so clearly seeing one client who was struggling to find her why, her purpose in life. I could see it was to create. A funny thing, though, is I could tell her this over and over again, but it was her journey to find it. She had to invest in herself and make the time to explore and get there. When she did, she was ecstatic. She was elated to share with me that she discovered her purpose, and it made everything in her life more meaningful, more connected. As she grew, her purpose didn't change, but it evolved as well.

Benefit 3 – It helps build courage and confidence.

One of the most rewarding pieces in my life has been seeing others as they invest in their growth become leaders with more courage and with more confidence in their skills and abilities. They would share how they didn't think they could ever have the tough conversation they just had, but they did it. It didn't happen overnight. They had a plan, worked on their skills, and exercised courage to step into the unknown because they wanted to address the person or process and feel the peace that came along with having a courageous conversation. With growing their skills and working on their development, they stepped into courage and through the courage, they built up their confidence. As this cycle continued in other areas, they started to see the connection in multiple areas of their lives.

What's holding you back from stepping into the benefits of growth and development? What's stopping you from incorporating that sacred time into your daily life? Remember, when I ask any question, I mean for you to reflect and answer it with intent, meaning, and purpose. This is part of filling in the shell of being a Peaceful Powered Leader. This book has little meaning if you aren't taking action, answering questions, completing the exercises, and spending time in reflection.

Sacred Time Discipline #3 – Invest, Instead of Spending

Throughout the years, I've struggled with this particular sacred time discipline. It wasn't until the last half decade I really explored what could happen in my life if I chose to explore how I was using my time. What I found was I was doing a lot of spending and very little investing. Let's first examine the difference in those two words. To spend means to use. We most often think of spending in terms of money. When we are spending our money, we are using it to purchase services or goods. We can spend money in a large scope of ways just like we can spend our time in many ways.

We can spend time watching television or movies. We can spend time surfing the Internet or on social media. We can spend time playing fantasy football and watching football games. We can spend time discussing why we don't need to use TPS reports at work. We can spend time discussing why Dave in finance is a pain to communicate with and why Danielle in IT always leads with, "Did you turn it off and turn it on again?" as the go-to response each time I call the help desk to get my computer fixed. The list is endless. We can always find ways to spend our time, because when we are spending, there usually isn't a clear purpose toward a higher goal or specific direction. The list, though, is different when we look at investing.

Investing, as in investing money, means being deliberate with our financial resources with an intent to grow them. We pay attention to how we invest. We usually have a clear goal and focus when we invest. It takes time, energy, and research to invest in smart ways. The spectrum for investments versus spending is much more detailed and focused. With investing, people usually expect a return. However, many know that with investment also comes loss or what one may consider failure at times.

Let's look at investing from a time perspective. When I invest, I am being deliberate with my time. I want my time to mean something. I want it to perhaps grow into something greater. I'm not just reading a book. I have a plan for why I am reading the book and a next action step upon completing it. I'm spending money to go to a seminar because it aligns with a three-year goal I am working toward, and I've already invested time in ensuring I am ready to take clear action steps from my learnings at the seminar.

Think of this very simple example between spending and investing our time. A person on one side of the bed wakes up, grabs their phone, and spends twenty-five minutes browsing the news, social media, sports scores, and more before ever getting out of bed. A person on the other side of the bed wakes up at the same time, gets dressed to work out, grabs their phone, starts an audiobook and goes for a twenty-five-minute run. There is a difference between the two in their approach to time.

The one going for the twenty-five-minute run is investing their time in their body. Depending on whether they are actively listening to the book and have potential focus for the book, one could argue they are investing in their mental well-being at the same time as their physical well-being. Let me be clear that I am not judging either person who lies in that bed. However, I want you to do some self-reflection on how you are incorporating sacred time with yourself and what type of work you are putting in to ensure your time has the focus you want and you are investing versus spending. Let's look at some ways to invest in yourself and how we can tie them together to get the returns you want.

Set goals.

Goal setting is the first step to investing versus spending. When you have documented goals, you have the ability to take action and connect your time to those goals. Don't just write your goals down, though. Research and review how to go from the end to the beginning with your goals. Lay out the framework.

One of the most eye-opening lessons about goals I learned from a coach was about professional golfers. A former coach shared with me how professional golfers don't shoot one shot at a time to get the ball in the hole. They, instead, have studied the course. They know each hole and the setup for that day. They know how many shots it takes to get par and where their strengths lie to gain greater movement on their goals and get birdies. They work backwards from the hole going from shot five all the way to one. They know the way they visualize it won't always go as planned, but they are prepared. If shot two doesn't land where they anticipated, they don't freak out and change their whole approach. They simply correct the next shot to get back on track. They don't allow a pebble to become a boulder. The more work we do up front with our goals, the greater returns we'll receive on the investment in our sacred time with ourselves.

Develop a reading plan.

Reading plans are a must for development. Reading can be pleasurable. It can also be focused. In 2018, I had a goal to read one book a week. Up to that year, I was an avid reader and read between twenty to thirty books some years. I did learn some, but my focus was sporadic. Sometimes books were connected to a goal, sometimes a book was a recommendation, and sometimes it was just a random pick. I actually read fifty-eight books by the time January 1, 2019 hit.

I wasn't reading just to finish, though. I was reading to learn and was deliberate in about forty-five of the fifty-eight books I selected to read. The other thirteen I did leave for random picks and recommendations. The forty-five, though, were part of a reading plan that connected to investment in my growth goals. That reading catapulted my progress like nothing had before. What I learned through my reading strengthened me as a coach, speaker, mentor, and leader in numerous ways. The reading also opened much easier routes to achieving my goals than I had anticipated. Additionally, reading was a much more enjoyable process because it was connected to a purpose. There was a great sense of learning and accomplishment from it.

Learn from others.

A new way to invest in learning that has grown popular over the last few years is through podcasts. I remember having an idea years ago after watching some inspiring TED Talks to create a social platform to allow people who were providing talks and sharing knowledge to be more accessible on a larger scale and for their audience to have the ability to reach out and ask questions. It was a way to take the traditional classroom and put it into people's hands with the social media boom in a more relaxed environment than someone speaking from a stage.

Like many ideas before, I talked about it, did a little research, but didn't work to move the action forward. I've changed this approach over the years as I've grown. Thankfully, the idea I envisioned was already in the works—podcasts. They are convenient to access and, when well produced, hold your attention. You can find a podcast to learn about almost anything you could imagine.

One of my favorite podcasts is Lewis Howes's "The School of Greatness." He was intentional in using the word "school," as each learning session provides a wealth of knowledge and ways to make the learning actionable. He often has guests who you would normally have to pay hundreds to thousands of dollars to hear at a conference or to talk with in a one-on-one coaching session.

Over the years, I feel I've acquired a minor in finance, a major in coaching, and a minor in marketing simply from listening to podcasts and taking action on the insights and lessons provided. I don't have a piece of paper that says I acquired these things, like I do for my undergrad and graduate degrees, but rest assured, I know I have them. I deliberately tied the podcasts I chose to my growth goals to invest my time rather than spend it. Just like with choosing books that further your goals, do your research to find out what podcasts will bring you the most value and how you can capitalize on the wellness run or drive to work to use the learning opportunity to its fullest potential.

Find seminars and workshops.

So many believe that they must go to a national workshop or seminar in a packed stadium or theater to get access to top-level development teachers and methods. Many people fail to realize they can find these resources in their own cities where attending may be free or a fraction of the cost of traveling to a large conference. Also, wonderful developers, like Brenè Brown and Cy Wakeman, have made their material available by directly certifying others to deliver it, so more people have access to high-value development tools without paying high-dollar costs. You just have to search for it!

I was lucky enough to spend time with Brenè and Cy, both of whom are *New York Times* bestsellers and world-renowned speakers, and to become certified in some of their material. I remember sitting with between eighty and ninety people with Brenè and just realizing the amount of amazing talent there is in this world. Most of the people in the room were providing workshops and seminars in their hometowns across the United States and abroad. They were people you and I had never heard of, but they were highly skilled and delivering their own well-researched content to those around them and becoming certified in Brenè's content to bring to others too.

Find those people in your community. Look for those offering learning opportunities that connect back to your goals and your desired growth and step into the lessons they have to offer. These investments go a long way but, unfortunately, most people don't make them a priority.

A recent study showed that the average American worker spends almost nine hours a day working, eight hours a day sleeping, three hours a day on sports and leisure, one hour a day eating and drinking, almost one hour a day on home chores, and almost half an hour each on shopping and taking care of family members.[9] You'll notice those numbers add up to twenty-three hours, and nowhere in there is growth and development mentioned. I couldn't verify growth and development was not included in the work data, but considering that LinkedIn's 2018 Workforce Learning Report states 94 percent of employees would stay at a company longer if it invested in their careers, I'm going to conclude that most people would say they were not engaging in growth and development at work.[10]

Monitor and challenge your mindset.

Acknowledge your emotions in pursuit of happiness. Part of developing sacred time for yourself and investing in yourself is being aware of your mindset and your emotions. One of the leaders who taught me the power of owning my mindset, and the reality that comes along with it is Cy Wakeman and her work around Reality-Based Leadership.

For years, I explored accountability and grew stronger and stronger in pieces of it. One area I continued to struggle heavily in was supplying fake details to fill in situations that occurred in my life. If my leader wanted to meet with me and didn't say why, I'd fill in the details that it was for something bad. If a friend didn't text back for a few days, I'd allow myself to come to the conclusion they may be mad at me. These were all stories, not accountable facts, and while I thought I was pretty accountable across some aspects of my life, Wakeman's education around Reality-Based Leadership helped me identify I had a problem with storytelling. I learned how to challenge my mindset in these areas, and I came to the realization that I had the power to be accountable and own my thoughts just like I did with the other pieces of my reality.

It is vital to monitor and challenge your mindset. Are you filling in fake details in lieu of firm facts? How can you work to change this? What would life be like if you consistently stuck to facts? This is one of the few times I'll provide an answer to a question I asked. Life is much more peaceful when we consistently stick to firm facts. It involves far less stress and worrying about the unknown.

Invest in a coach.

While spending sacred time with yourself may sound like a solo activity, this is one piece of investing in yourself that can involve another person. The international coach federation (ICF) defines coaching as a partnering with clients in a thought-provoking and creative process that inspires them to maximize their personal and professional potential. I love this definition, as it has been my experience as both a certified coach and as a client working with a coach.

While we may think we know ourselves well, a coach is someone dedicated to a partnership with you. They are listening to where you want to take your development and providing thought-provoking questions to help get you there. They partner to set up action steps and build a process that keeps you investing in yourself in the ways you want if you are accountable to the process. Each coaching session can be a strong way to invest in a focused effort toward development.

Make time for strategy thinking.

Sacred time with yourself allows for forward movement and provides a huge investment opportunity. One of the biggest pitfalls I've seen leaders struggle to overcome is just working from one day to the next in decision-making and taking action. It doesn't matter what level of leadership they are involved in; this is a chronic problem for many leaders. Why is this? When you aren't setting aside sacred time to reflect, you are only strategizing in meetings that allow for it. And guess what? Those meetings aren't too productive because most people aren't ready to think strategy in them. They are pulling ideas out that are usually half-built on something someone else brought up in the meeting. They are thinking about preparing for their next meeting.

Sacred time for reflection allows people, if they work to develop it into their routine, to think about the future. How are the decisions I am going to make this week going to affect those I lead, myself, and others in my life next week, next month, next year, and so on? Those who reflect regularly aren't thinking of their next move on the fly. They have already thought about multiple potential moves, and depending on what is coming their way, they can, with a clear head, decide what to do next. They've already reviewed the outcome they want to achieve. They've worked backwards step by step to play out what they are planning for and even if one step goes astray, we know they just have to course correct that piece, but they are still ready for the next.

Making time to invest in strategy helps prepare us for next steps and allows peace to be maintained while we watch others around us scramble because they are spending their time on the now while you invested time long ago in the now for today!

Celebrate what you are doing.

I often ask people how they celebrated after they accomplished something small or large. Rather routinely, I'll get a confused look, a pause, and a response along the lines of, "This wasn't a huge accomplishment, and I don't do a big celebration just for something like this." Their mind almost always, in my interactions, goes to "celebration is a big thing."

Just a little progress day after day adds up to big things. However, people rarely celebrate the little progress. Invest in your progress and make a memory of the moment by celebrating with yourself over a cup of tea in a quiet place or sitting by a stream on a park bench. In the moment, though, be intentional with your purpose. "Today I sit on this park bench because I finished part three of my ten-part project. No one knows this but me, and I'm okay with that. What went well with this part of the project? Did I learn some things I need to apply in my next steps? I did well and I am going to take a moment to recognize myself."

You see, the celebration isn't always a huge party, but it should exist. We often miss these moments for ourselves, and in turn, we also miss providing them for those we lead. Make the investment of celebration a part of your life by being deliberate in establishing ways you like to celebrate the small forward progress and the big achievements! It helps keep things in perspective and allows us to not get lost in the end result and stay present in the journey along the way. It is rare for people to truly believe in themselves and work to ensure they don't put limits on themselves.

If you are moving forward, not allowing yourself to be bound by limiting beliefs, whether success or failure, celebrate! You are approaching situations with, "I am doing this, and I will!" You break through any limiting beliefs that may be there on a regular basis for so many, and you are trying. With that approach, no matter the outcome, you can be at peace, already knowing you have won because you've stepped into something the majority, unfortunately, aren't willing to do in life. You invested in yourself and you tried. Trying is the real measure of success.

Getting Your Calendar in Check Exercise

I hope after reading the ways to invest in yourself, you are itching for the opportunity to start being more consistent about it, if you're not already. Start now with this calendar exercise, which will also help you build in time for reflection and detachment, if you choose to make it happen.

Step 1: Pull up your calendar for the next month.

If you are like me, you've got most meetings set up at least six to eight weeks in advance, not including your recurring meetings. So start looking for open spots—times when there are no recurring meetings. You may already have a one-time meeting in some of these spots over the next month, but you know it is usually open until the next month of meetings starts to get scheduled. Don't let those one-time meetings keep you from plugging in a permanent, recurring meeting going forward.

Step 2: Find the time to book some meetings with yourself.

Now go through each week and look for anywhere to block out time with yourself. Your goal is between two and eight hours of sacred time each week. And remember, this can be during your normal work schedule or off hours or weekends. If you truly care about your development, you'll schedule time with yourself on the weekends too. Think about this: If you are scheduling eight hours a week of sacred time to invest and investing that time with deliberate intention, you are going to have thirty-two to forty hours of development time each month. I feel confident sharing with you that you will thank yourself for this, your team members will thank you, and your organization will thank you in multiple ways because of the type of leadership you will bring forward. Your return will be so much greater than if you had chosen to spend your time rather than investing it consistently in your development.

People seem to struggle most with scheduling sacred time "meetings" during work hours. Many have failed this exercise because they haven't had a mindset shift in how an appointment works. If someone books an appointment, the intent is to keep it, regardless of who it is with. If the appointment is with yourself, the time is blocked. Don't schedule over it because you received a short turnaround meeting request from someone else.

Many times, I've had someone say, "I've got to get on your schedule this week!" When I ask for an agenda for what they want to accomplish and why they have to get on my schedule, they tell me what the meeting is about, but offer no agenda. Guess what, I'm not going to spend my time that way. They are shuffling, not strategizing. If I don't have the time available because I have an appointment with myself or a one-on-one with a team member, I don't move those appointments for this person who couldn't develop an agenda for us.

Too often leaders will move a one-on-one with a team member who is looking so forward to meeting with them for someone who is perceived as being more important. Leaders are even quicker to cancel their appointments with themselves. ***Stop!*** This is sacred time for your team member and you in a one-on-one, and it is sacred time for your growth in how you can best invest in others and yourself. Keep these appointments.

Step 3: Book a recurring meeting with yourself for development.

This is an easy step in the process. What is not easy for people is shifting their mind to these appointments being real appointments. Setting up a recurrence makes it a little more real because it is locked in on your calendar. It is one more step toward consistency. That block is no longer available on your calendar. It is now up to you to be disciplined and keep it that way. I've found that when those people claiming they need time on your calendar come forward, they also usually want you to fit time around their schedule. This leads us to Step 4.

Step 4: Get in the habit of providing options.

When someone comes forward with a proposed meeting time that doesn't work for you, let them know, but provide some alternative options. People are too willing to push aside their sacred investment time for a short-notice meeting over simply saying, "I'm booked during that time, but here are three options. Please let me know if any work for you, or if we need to look at some other times."

People are afraid of the judgment that may come with saying no to a meeting. Guess what, though, the process I just described isn't a no. Instead, it's an approach that allows for mutual respect and collaboration. No one can claim you weren't accommodating. You provided three times and offered to look beyond that if that didn't work for them. What you didn't do was compromise your sacred time with yourself or those you lead. Start working to make this a habit.

Step 5: Evaluate your value add and mission essential reasons for being at group meetings.

When people outside of those you lead approach you for a one-on-one meeting, it can be easy to use the habit in Step 4. People have shared with me that they struggle more with keeping an appointment with themselves when they are asked to attend a larger group meeting, usually run by someone with a peer title or above. This step goes directly back to the foundation of becoming a Peaceful Powered Leader—own and set your reality. If you are going to a two-hour meeting every other week where you are only asked to provide value for five minutes, it is time to have a conversation with the meeting organizer.

Discuss with them some alternative solutions of how the value you add to the meeting could be done in a written form you provide ahead of the meeting for someone to share, or how you could be more instrumental in providing value to the meeting. But stop going to the meeting unless your part in it changes. Take some time and go through your meetings and reflect on the purpose each one serves. Is it a meeting that brings value for your team and you? Does it connect strongly to the mission, purpose, and actions your team has been asked to strive for? Are you capturing valuable notes to share with your team that engages them and you in different ways?

Or does the meeting feel like a "check the box" process when you attend? Is it of value? How often do you find yourself bringing back vital information or ideas to share with your team? Is it a meeting that is being regularly moved and causes you to reschedule important time with those you lead? Negotiate to no longer spend time going to the Low Value Add and Low Mission Essential meetings or negotiate what needs to change in your role in these meetings that would move them to more High Mission Essential or High Value Add experiences. This may require a courageous conversation, but that short conversation can open the door to better time invested in one way or another.

Go through these steps, taking the time to reflect on and evaluate the types of meetings you are attending and the value they bring to your team, including you. Doing this review on a recurring three- to six-month basis is a vital part of leadership. Leaders I've coached over the years often have said they need more time, but the reality for most people is they need to be more effective with their time and more comfortable in how they say yes and no to where their time goes. If we are spending day after day putting out fires in business or other areas of our life, remember, you have the power to change this. You have the power to make deliberate and actionable changes to ensure you are developing sacred time with yourself. When we miss setting and investing in sacred time with ourselves, it can be hard to bring our best selves to everyone else we interact with.

If you aren't happy serving those you lead, you have the power to change this. Take care of yourself through your sacred time, so you can also take care of those you lead. Your well-being must be a priority for you, and it's important you take the time to find out the right way to be healthy in your self-care. I once had a friend who looked great physically but shared with me that they absolutely hated their running and workout routine. I asked them why they continued it and they said, "Because it works." I asked them what they meant by this and they went on to explain that they had the body they wanted. I then asked, "Could you still have the body you want and do a routine you enjoyed?" As we talked further, they shared they had made this routine a habit and hadn't thought about changing it. Some habits we may need to break, whether they are physical or mental, in order to spend sacred time with ourselves. This friend took our talk to heart and started looking for a new way to invest in their well-being that provided a different outlet. They were no longer thinking about how miserable they were in their workout but instead having peaceful reflection as they embraced their well-being routine in a new way, as part of their sacred time. What was that new routine you may be asking? This friend took up mountain biking and continued to love the way they looked physically but also shared that they thoroughly enjoyed their workout time now. It allowed them to reflect and spend sacred time with themselves in a new way.

As I've shared before, this book is not a clear-cut how-to guide, because each journey is different. I can tell you it takes action to find the right sacred time practices for you. You have to put in the effort to explore what works and along the way figure out what doesn't. Some exploring may be easy, while other pieces will probably be seriously hard. Either way, the cool part to keep in mind is the journey is ultimately leading to peace.

Chapter 6
Peaceful Powered Leaders Empower Themselves and Create an Environment for Others to Succeed

mpowerment seems to be a tricky topic for a lot of leaders and organizations. I've experienced a company where the word "empowerment" was barely used but clearly it was being exercised at every level. On the other hand, I've known an organization where the CEO constantly used the word to remind everyone how empowered they were without actually describing what that meant or how it was scoped for them to own it. The outcome was one of the least empowered organizations I've had contact with because people weren't sure where that empowerment began and ended and were afraid to exercise the power they owned.

Empowerment, in my experience, tends to be easy to step into when it is talked about and scoped, much like trust conversations. Trust between people is rarely discussed, but it should be. Trust is different from one relationship to the next, and the boundaries associated with trust in a particular relationship can grow and change over time. Empowerment works in a similar way, and because trust is a big connecter to empowerment, I want to start by exploring trust and then build to discussing empowerment and its companion thought process of giving people options instead of excuses and of opening the door for failure and success through trying!

The Trust Factor

Trust is a part of any relationship. Let's take a moment to look at the first five parts of becoming a Peaceful Powered Leader and how trust is a factor in each one. First, we explored owning and setting your reality. This is part of the relationship with yourself and building self-trust in how you approach things and make decisions with an ownership mentality. Building on that piece as the foundation, a Peaceful Powered Leader can step into building others up.

Building others up is centered around both self-trust and trust with others. As you build others up, you work to own your ego and understand that you are good enough. You don't hesitate to put the attention on someone else, because you understand you are in charge of your outcomes and giving someone else a boost, a credit, or attention doesn't hinder you; it only opens the door to extend and build trust with others. Your focus on them is coming with positive intent and as you create a pattern of this behavior, people will see that words and actions go hand and hand with you. This is a formula for building trust with others.

Serving others in lieu of making self-serving decisions at the expense of others, again, builds on self-trust. It creates consistency for you that you are able to own and hold true to your values. Again, this is rooted in owning your reality and the outcomes associated with that reality. Not only does this piece build self-trust, but it again extends trust with others as they see your actions match your words and how those connect to your values. From here, Peaceful Powered Leaders work to invest in others.

Investing in others comes in many forms, shapes, and sizes. It can be met with hesitation if others question your intent. However, if you are leading with ownership of self, building others up, and making decisions based on values that honor service to others in leadership over self-serving decisions, you are walking on a path that allows people to see your reality of positive intent toward others. That opens the door to invest in others and for them to step into the investment you are helping them with. This is a big piece in also opening the door to empowerment. As we invest in others, they grow, and the scope of their confidence grows with them. As a leader, to continue helping others grow, you, too, must invest in yourself.

Investment in self through sacred time can be a struggle if you aren't owning your reality. However, when ownership of reality occurs, people understand they can't get where they want to go for themselves and in pursuit of helping others without putting the work in. That work can often be uncomfortable as we are in the process of growing. Investment in ourselves is a reminder that we understand and believe in our worth. We know we are good enough to help ourselves and others. We are continuing to build our self-trust and modeling the way for people to trust us. We have put the time, energy, and effort into ourselves to be able to happily and healthily help others. When these pieces all come together, you have molded a model for empowerment of self and others.

While each element in the process of becoming a Peaceful Powered Leader opens the door to both self-trust and trust with others, it is important to talk about trust and explore it as its own subject. Document in your journaling or take time in self-reflection to capture how you are building upon or sustaining your self-trust. If you have faltered—because we are humans, we make mistakes—capture what growth you've learned from the experience. Is there a way to work toward ensuring it will be harder to falter next time?

Talk to people in relationships with you about trust. As stated earlier, a major component of trust is boundaries. Boundaries change when people make investments in relationships and also when people make withdrawals. Withdrawals don't mean a total loss of trust, but the relationship may look and feel different because of new boundaries. When boundaries change, and the topic goes undiscussed, it can easily lead to conflict and bigger trust withdrawals occurring than we intended or realized. Visit boundaries regularly in relationships to discuss if they are expanding or decreasing. This applies to any area of our lives. Let's use an example of a relationship with a child.

I currently have a thirteen-year-old son, who is just finishing seventh grade. He is very responsible from a rules perspective. The first time we discussed letting him stay home alone for an hour while we ran errands was a trust and empowerment conversation. We didn't just tell him a set list of rules. It was a partnership conversation. We discussed the rules and talked with him about why he believed those rules were in place. We wanted to make sure he understood he was being empowered and how that empowerment was scoped. We wanted him to know how we got to this place of trust.

When he shared with us how he understood why we trusted him and the empowerment he was taking ownership of, we felt clear boundaries were established. As the hour rule of being home alone went well time and time again, we sat down and had another conversation about extending the trust boundary in this area to two hours. I'm sure many people can relate to this example. It is a conversation and a partnership, and it is no different in the workplace. Unfortunately, though, the conversation is often bypassed due to lack of time, planning, or understanding. It is imperative we make time to discuss trust, the boundary points in each relationship, and the empowerment in it.

This brings us to our next topic and a key sentence I hope you remember and work to apply as you embrace Peaceful Powered Leadership going forward:

Empowerment can't only be given; it also has to be taken.

In the opening to this section, I referenced an organization where the CEO shared that all were empowered. However, that empowerment wasn't scoped in a way that people understood how they were empowered or where the boundaries were, so they didn't explore how to take hold of it. They were afraid to experiment and just left the power alone. They felt safer this way, while expressing extensively how they wished they were empowered to own their work and do what was right by the customers. Where was the disconnect here? Ownership!

The CEO thought he was giving something that he owned to the people he led, but the reality is, empowerment has to be taken. Empowerment is all around us if we are looking for it. It can be much easier to step into if someone is laying out how to do that with us in partnership, but even if that reality doesn't currently exist for you, it doesn't mean empowerment opportunities aren't available.

Peaceful Powered Leaders look for and take empowerment opportunities. They also work to be clear in laying out the opportunities available to those they lead. As a leader, helping someone step into empowerment can take time to do effectively, but the reality that comes into play when those you lead and partner with are taking that step is an amazing place to be. This part of becoming a Peaceful Powered Leader ties directly into setting and owning your reality. The following practices are designed to complement the work you've accomplished so far and build upon the structures you've put in place if you've made the choice to be active in your growth.

Giving People Options, Not Excuses

Empowerment focuses on what can be accomplished instead of what can't. I've encountered leaders and entire teams that are really good at giving excuses for why something can't be accomplished. However, circling back to the very first piece of becoming a Peaceful Powered Leader, owning and setting your reality, will change this. When someone owns their reality and the understanding that every next step, every choice, is theirs to own, they aren't waiting for solutions to drop into their lap. They are looking for ways to make their next step happen, and they find options.

When a leader is thinking this way, they are asking themselves questions. How can I make this happen? What can I do to own this next move and get that much closer to where I want to be? Great leaders stop trying to give others answers and instead empower them to take hold of the ownership they already possess by asking them the right questions. When we help ourselves and others learn to be better questioners, instead of answerers, we step into a whole new arena of options, instead of excuses.

"If I had an hour to solve a problem, I'd spend fifty-five minutes thinking about the problem and five minutes thinking about solutions." This quote from Albert Einstein captures the true essence of questioning. Einstein was explaining the importance of really understanding what we are looking at. When we understand it, solutions become much easier to find. We aren't stepping into action bias, trying to do something only to show forward movement or productivity. We instead are taking the time to question the challenge in front of us. Eventually, we will understand it, and this will open the door for real root cause solutions to come forward.

So often though, if people don't see the answer right in front of them, or it can't be achieved the way they thought it could, excuses start to roll off the tongue. Peaceful Powered Leaders don't allow this to be the norm. Instead, they challenge their thought process and the thought process of others through questioning and seeking out what accountability in the situation looks like.

I remember being around a senior leader who would tell anyone who would listen how she was excluded by the rest of the senior leaders she worked with. If two of her peers were talking about something that she didn't know about but felt she should have, she would ask the following question: "Why doesn't anyone ever include me?" She would quickly provide the answer too: "Because they don't care about me. They are intentionally leaving me out." She'd stop there and usually show signs of visible frustration. I'm not joking when I say this senior leader would do this out loud in front of other people on a consistent basis.

Let's examine this senior leader's process. She would overhear peers talking about something she felt she should have been included in. What did she do? She'd ask why she wasn't included. This isn't a question phrased for someone to own. Instead it is a question that puts blame on others. She is going toward a victim process that will keep her out of solution-based thinking. She is going the route of finding an excuse. And rest assured, this happened to her over and over.

Imagine, instead, if she had said, "How can I ensure I am included so I can get this needed information I hear them talking about?" This question focuses on ensuring the person remains accountable for finding solutions. They are asking what action they can take to ensure they get the outcome they'd like to see. The answer to the question may be, "I have to go and talk with them and see how I can be included." I have given myself an answer that I can own. I have empowered myself to take next steps by asking an accountable question. Can you see the difference of having a focus on "How can I?" versus "Why is this happening to me?"

When we empower ourselves and others, we still must work to scope what the empowerment looks like. This helps build both our self-trust and trust with others (as we have previously focused on) but don't forget the other side of those parameters. When we scope something out, we are inviting ourselves or others to step into that path. We are extending trust to ourselves to go somewhere we may not have been before, but we know we are empowered to take the journey. We are opening the door for someone we lead to step into ownership of the empowerment we have scoped for them.

We can't make someone step into empowerment; that is their choice. We can, however, scope it, model it, and help them through questioning to find out why they haven't stepped into it yet. Once we help ourselves and others understand how we can own empowerment, it is time for us to become comfortable with failure. This is one of the last practices I will discuss in becoming a Peaceful Powered Leader, and I've left it for the end by design.

Failure is a word that is scary for many, especially if you have avoided activities that could lead to that outcome. If I had started out discussing failure as an essential piece of becoming a Peaceful Powered Leader, many readers would have put down the book. Most of us have been taught to fear failure, and it's difficult to let go of that concept.

In today's culture, though, a shift has been occurring. Some people are now trying to teach that failure is a good thing. It has actually become a stimulating word but still is only fully embraced by a few. Let's examine where we've come from since starting our journey to becoming a Peaceful Powered Leader. This is a big reason why I set up the parameters in the opening about doing the exercises as you went through the book and taking your time. The process was setting you up to become a Peaceful Powered Leader and be comfortable with failure.

Take a moment to reflect on the actions you've taken if you've reached this point in the book and gone through each of the exercises and learning pieces. Let's just recap some of the awesomeness you've accomplished and the foundation you've laid to build on. You worked through taking a deeper look at yourself and went into the reflection on how you currently are owning and setting your reality. You challenged yourself to go through question after question and be honest about where you were, why you were there, and how you would build. This took courage!

Next, you ventured into exploring how you show gratitude toward others and spend time building others up. You got real with yourself about what this process feels like and what it could become. You shifted to the reality you have full power to own and taken the reality forward to build others up. You worked on trust, both in your connections and how it impacts your ability to invest in others. This opened the door to self-reflection through journaling, reminding yourself to start with celebrating what is working well.

Upon building others up, you stepped into continuing to serve others and ensuring your self-interests weren't keeping you from sticking to your values. This piece was one of the toughest in my journey to becoming a Peaceful Powered Leader. As I shared, I found through this process that one of the values I wanted to be in my top three wasn't. This was a hard realization, but I knew it was mine to own and I could change it if I wanted. You may have had a moment or two like this, and now you've already got time set aside to start working on prioritizing your values because you took active steps in going through the calendar exercise and being deliberate about building in sacred time for yourself. You have the opportunity built into your schedule now to grow and develop if you choose to.

In doing all this, you took steps to grow. Remember, growing takes time. Building lifestyle changes usually takes between sixty to ninety days, and we still struggle at times, and that is okay. You've worked to build a foundation of peace in your leadership. A foundation that includes service to others in multiple ways and honoring yourself in the process.

I'm reminding you of all this because with the door to courage opened, you have also opened the door to failure. This is a door I hope you celebrate reaching while being ready to embrace the spectrum of emotions that comes with it. Choosing courage over comfort is the tipping point to feeling comfortable with failure, just maybe not in the way some have shared it before.

Opening Up the Door for Failure

For a long time, I felt that failure was at one end of the ruler and success was at the other end. Then, one day, it was as if someone smacked me in the head with that ruler and I saw a completely different ruler. This ruler didn't have the words success or failure on it. It only had one word written all over it: Try! It wasn't written at each measurement on the ruler either. In fact, this ruler didn't have measurements on it. It was just a piece of wood that had "try" written all over it.

Some of the "trys" were written really large, clearly by someone who had a lot of confidence in the word. Some were written extremely small, almost as if the writer wasn't sure it was okay to write on the ruler, but they were still going to take a chance. There were scribbled "trys" that looked like they were written by someone very tired, who had just enough energy left to print the word on the ruler. I also saw "try" written neatly and clearly with creative stenciling, as if the writer had planned out how to present the word and ensured they had plenty of time to get it just right.

I didn't know which versions of the word came along with success or failure. I just knew one thing: All of these people had tried and that was pretty awesome because I knew how hard it had been to try at different points in my life. I also realized that trying was a part of me empowering myself, and that in the workplace when my team members tried, it appeared to be a lot easier for them when I helped them understand it was okay to fail and it was okay to succeed, just as long as they were trying.

Have you ever opened the door to failure? If you have ever tried something new, you have. Guess what, you also, whether realizing it or not, opened the door to success at the same time. Again, when we own our reality, we set the stage to step into empowerment. I remember the first time I was wrestling with the idea of opening the door to an external professional coaching practice.

I had spent almost two years working toward gaining my Associate Certified Coach designation through the International Coach Federation with a goal of becoming a certified coach and having my own external practice separate from the organizations I was working in. It took a lot of time, energy, and effort to get there, and I finally got the certification. I then did the work to set up my own practice. It came time to advertise for clients, but I couldn't do it. I wouldn't ask myself why because I didn't want to own the reality of the answer. I told myself I had the courage to get my coaching certification, which took a lot of time, energy, and resources.

One day, I was on the phone with a long-distance friend. I shared with her all the preparation I had done to develop a coaching welcome packet, an intake form, advertisement sheets, and so forth. She then asked the question I had been avoiding, "So when are you going to start advertising?" I told her I wasn't sure, and she asked why. I told her, again, I wasn't sure and that the timing didn't feel right. This person was a vital friend and knew me well. She proceeded to ask a more direct question, "I can hear in your voice something holding you back. What is it?"

I knew there was trust and lack of judgment with this vital friend, so I shared with her, "I'm afraid. I'm afraid I'll be judged. What I advertise may not be good enough."

I was so relieved to have said it out loud. This wonderful friend reminded me of all the trying I had done to get to that point. She also reminded me that I could potentially fail and succeed as I continued to try, and that was okay. As we talked, she didn't empower me, because only I could do that, but she helped me scope out what trying looked like around my coaching practice. I realized I may be judged, and I may fail, but that I also may succeed. Either route was okay because I was trying, and I was trying something I was really passionate about.

I stepped into the empowerment I owned and, before I knew it, I had my first three external coaching clients. It was a great feeling. The funny thing was that as I stepped into this empowerment, I put my emphasis on trying. I didn't put parameters on what success looked like, other than I wanted to have coaching clients. Success wasn't four or six or eight clients. It was trying. The ruler had truly changed. Before I knew it, I had more clients than I could handle since I was only doing the external practice as a side gig and I still had another full-time job.

My friend didn't empower me, but she helped me see the empowerment I could step into. This is a key distinction I want you to recognize as a Peaceful Powered Leader. We must own our reality and step into our empowerment, while working to create an environment for those we lead where they can step into their empowerment too. If you've built the other areas of becoming a Peaceful Powered Leader—owning and setting your reality, building others up, serving others before self, investing in others and yourself through sacred time—then you've set the scoping for creating an environment of empowerment. Sharing all this, though, can be much easier than truly becoming comfortable with failure. Being deliberate in how we identify growth in failure can make the process more comfortable.

Identify the value of failure.

Let's be clear: People don't usually want to fail. They may say they are okay with failing, but that doesn't mean they don't want to succeed. It's important to understand what failure means to you. Part of this understanding comes from being comfortable knowing you could fail and identifying the value that comes out of it. We should be deliberate in identifying how we failed, why we may have failed, and how we can grow from it, to ensure we capture the value of it.

When a reporter famously asked the question "How does it feel to fail one thousand times?" of Thomas Edison, his response captured how he ensured there was value in his failures. He responded, "I didn't fail one thousand times. The lightbulb was an invention with one thousand steps." Thomas Edison knew failure was a possibility with each try of inventing the lightbulb. He also scoped out how to find value in the failure, knowing that try number 99 or 999 could be the success he was looking for, and if it wasn't, he was going to document why and re-examine possible next steps. He was living the quote famously said decades later by businessperson Sumner Redstone, "Success is not built on success. It's built on failure. It's built on frustration. Sometimes it's built on catastrophe."

I share Redstone's quote because many organizations and influencers have tried to make failure sexy. When I share that it's important to become comfortable with failure and learn to find the value in it, make no mistake: Failure is often hard to handle, but it is okay, as long as we keep trying.

Break through ego and shame.

Many people struggle to step into empowerment because of fears. Fears that are rooted in ego and shame. My story of being nervous about advertising my coaching practice for the first time was full of ego and shame. I had been very successful as a leader and development consultant inside an organization. I, however, had a lot to learn about doing that work outside that sphere as a small business owner. My ego was afraid to fail. I was afraid of what others might say and the shame failure would bring. The deciding factor in not letting the ego and shame reign supreme, came down to one simple piece: my purpose.

Remember when I shared that the best leaders don't give the answer, but they instead ask questions? Asking questions is also a great way to shed the negativity brought on by our ego and the shame we perceive will be associated with failure. When fear of failure starts to set in, question why. Let's go through the following exercise to explore. I'll use my external coaching practice as an example.

Question 1: Why am I afraid to advertise amongst friends, family, and former colleagues about my new external coaching practice?
Answer 1: I'm afraid of being judged.

Question 2: Why am I afraid of being judged?
Answer 2: Because of my ego. I want to be thought of as successful right now.

Question 3 and 4: Why is success important to me? What was the purpose of me getting my coaching certification?
Answers 3 and 4: My purpose in life is to help others grow and develop and inspire them to take action. I got my coaching certification to be able to help others grow and develop and inspire them to take action. Success is helping others grow and develop and inspiring them to take action. I am making this about me and not about my purpose and how it is associated with helping others.

Question 5: How do I move forward in this process to help others grow and develop and inspire them to take action?

Answer 5: I advertise my external coaching practice because it's not about me; it's about helping others in new ways.

Do you see what happened there? Through the power of questioning, I brought my ego and shame into the light. I was making the coaching practice about me and I lost sight of why I was working toward it in the first place. Yes, others may judge me, and I may fail. However, I hold the key to empowering myself to move forward into next steps. I also have a key that could unlock a door for others to step forward into their empowerment through the coaching help I could potentially provide.

Bringing our ego and shame to light helps break down the case our ego is trying to make and the shame it is carrying in the briefcase with it. It took me incorporating into my growth plan active steps to question myself when I moved to fear of failure and ultimately fear of trying. Stop now and take a moment to examine the action plan you've hopefully been building as you've spent time reading through the pages of this book. Ask yourself the following questions, and make sure you reflect before each answer. Take your time. This isn't a quick exercise, and it is a process that you will want to work to hardwire.

1. Do I wrestle with my ego? If so, how do I recognize I am in a match with my ego?

2. Does my ego and the shame it brings forward keep me from trying at times?

3. How can I do a better job of identifying when my ego is hiding in the dark and needs to be brought into the light?

4. What measures can I put in place when I start to realize this is happening, so I can bring my ego to light?

5. How can I ensure I will be actionable in next steps, try, and step into the empowerment I own when I've called out my ego and the shame it is sometimes carrying with it?

6. What fears do I have about trying the process I've laid out for calling out my ego and being active in trying even when my ego is pulling me to do otherwise?

7. Do I need a support partner at times for this process? If so, what are some support practices I would like from them? (Good support partners could be professional coaches, therapists, vital friends, a supportive leader, or a combination of these.)

Once you've worked through this process, the next part is acting on it. I am very deliberate in my purpose to help others grow and develop and inspire them to take action. The last piece, to take action, I added after years of being an adult educator.

I would facilitate a learning session and have numerous people tell me how motivating it was and that they were excited to use what they learned. I was happy for them in the moment. Then I would follow up with them a month or two later to find out how things were going, and they would share with me that they, unfortunately, hadn't taken any action with the material and foundational learning that had occurred. Their investment stopped in the facilitated session. They had positive intent to use the material but oftentimes struggled to act on it. Many times, this was because they had been taught that in order to make changes in their growth and development, they needed a well-laid-out action plan. Let me debunk that myth right now. While well-laid-out action plans can be a great thing, they aren't a necessity.

I fell in love with author Mel Robbins's *5 Second Rule* because she caught the essence of action. She shared that we could use the countdown "5, 4, 3, 2, 1, go!" in order to keep moving forward toward goals. It doesn't matter if we don't have the perfect shorts, shirt, or shoes to go run our first mile of our workout plan, just start and pick those things up after the workout! It doesn't matter that we don't have a well-laid-out journal that has action-oriented questions or dates built in for our daily journaling project. Use a sticky note and start! Again, you can go get that fancy journal on your way home from work tonight. Just take action, one step at a time.

The ego will tell you that you aren't ready to go to the workout class because everyone there has the nice shirt, shoes, and shorts. Well, guess what? The class starts today. As long as you are there, taking the first steps on your workout journey, you are trying, and there is no shame in that. The people who are there for the right reasons will lift you up, regardless of you having the right tools to be there. Take action and keep taking action. Don't let the ego fool you and be resilient.

Bring forth resiliency and keep things in perspective.

As I was mapping out the pieces for this section, for some reason, each time I looked at the phrase "bring forth resiliency and keep things in perspective," the movie *Risky Business* with Tom Cruise kept jumping into my mind. Now, the movie itself is a pretty far-fetched reality; however, its message and learnings have been moving strong for over thirty-five years now. I share this because just the other day I sat down to watch a show on a children's network with my son, and they were doing a PG-rated remake of the movie in the episode. It had the same learning points, including a scene at the end where the mother called her son into the room to ask if he cracked her egg. In the children's show, it was an actual egg, versus in the movie where it was a crystal egg.

In the 1983 movie, Tom Cruise plays the character Joel. I am going to use the scene from the movie with Joel's father, which is a little bit tamer than the scene with Joel and his friend. Both scenes share the same point. Joel is talking with his father about some struggles he is going through and the challenges he is facing. As he is sharing, his father gives him one simple piece of advice, "Sometimes you gotta say, 'What the heck.'"

This advice kept ringing through my mind for this section. What Joel's father is sharing, from my interpretation of the scene, is be resilient and keep things in perspective. This attitude has a big role in breaking through our ego and shame as well. When we are equipped with processes to do this, it makes it easier to get to resiliency and keep things in perspective.

A big part of how we step into empowerment and become okay with failure is by being resilient. Resiliency is how we learn from failure. Often people associate resiliency with recovery. I want to challenge that mindset. When we think of recovering from failure, I believe it still ties us to the ruler with one end being failure and the other end being success.

Resiliency for Peaceful Powered Leaders is trying and having the willingness to keep trying. This can be hard at times; however, that is where the other part of this comes into play—keeping things in perspective.

The process of resiliency can be overwhelming at times and that is where the advice from *Risky Business* comes in, "Sometimes you gotta say, 'What the heck.'" I like to add to this, "Sometimes you gotta say, 'What the heck, let's take a break and have some fun.'"

Too often, in the workplace and in our lives in general, we miss out on having fun. Whose choice is this? Ours! It goes back to setting and owning our reality. I'm sure you can recall story after story of a business venture team that set out to have fun while working toward their goals, and somewhere along the way, it just became about getting to the goals. How do we ensure we don't lose sight of fun? Fun adds to the experience.

I remember the first trail run I ever ran. It was a 5K. I had run 5K's before but never on a trail. When I signed up for the run with two friends, I didn't bother to scope out the actual trail, and I quickly found out it was pretty intense for a first-time trail runner. It increased in elevation quickly, it was all single trail (meaning not a lot of foot space to run on), and I wasn't great at pacing myself at this point in my running pursuits. I was, however, resilient. I was determined to finish, but I wasn't having fun. As I followed behind my friend, back down the trail we had just run up—because the 5K required a turnaround at the halfway point—I wasn't embracing the experience. I just wanted to finish. That is when my friend said, "What the heck!"

She stopped me, took out her phone, and said, "Let's grab a selfie to capture this moment!" Right there, that people powered moment captured the perspective I had lost. I signed up for this race to have fun. In the moment, though, I was just focused on being resilient and wrestling with my ego to not quit and not look bad coming across the finish line. I lost the perspective of having fun, but thankfully my dear friend brought the fun back into perspective, and I had a smile on my face the rest of the race.

Fast-forward to just over two years later, and I was running the Apollo 11K on the road that leads into Kennedy Space Station. It was a scalding hot morning that didn't start off great for me. I had to drive about fifty minutes to the race from where I was visiting my parents. I was so excited for this race. It was in celebration of the fiftieth anniversary of the Apollo 11 space mission. I was going to arrive at 6:00 a.m. and the race started at 6:15.

As I was following my GPS in the dark, I realized I missed the turn for the parking. I was now driving on the road I was about to run on, and all the roundabouts were blocked off. I had to travel four miles to the next open roundabout. I was getting nervous I wouldn't make it in time to start with everyone else. I finally made it to the parking lot at 6:12. I parked in one of the only spots left, about a quarter of a mile from the starting line, and I booked it to the start of the race. It was about 95 degrees already.

As I approached the starting line, I heard the emcee state that they were running ten minutes behind. Whew! I was relieved. I was going to make the start on time. Before I knew it, we were off, and I realized I was running with the front 25 percent of the pack, and I kept inching closer and closer to the front of the pack. In the first mile, there was this cool Kennedy Space Station sign. I saw a few racers stop to take pictures. I thought to myself, "That'd be cool, but I am making great time and have to keep pushing forward." As I reached the turnaround for the 11K, I thought to myself, "Only about 10 percent of the runners are on their way back, and I know there are age-group awards for this race. I could get one!"

Here I was, again losing sight of perspective and just focusing on resiliency. I started to push forward. I was forgetting the why of doing this race: fun. As I approached the last mile, I knew I was close to the top three in my age group, and I had a lot left in my tank to sprint to the finish. As I was thinking about this, I saw the sign I passed at mile one. In that moment, I thought about my friend and our selfie on the trail run. It was the only time I had done that, and I had been in dozens of races. Perspective came back to me, and I reminded myself that I wanted to challenge myself and also have fun. I stopped and took a selfie at the sign. I was so glad to capture that moment. From there, I continued to sprint to the finish line, with about .85 miles to go. I finished and was so excited. Within about thirty minutes, I found out that I had gotten fourth in my age group, and I quickly realized the selfie cost me medaling.

The time between third place in my age group and my time was only seconds. In this moment, the thought could've passed through my head, "I shouldn't have stopped." However, that thought never entered into my mind. I was happy and at peace with my decision, because I kept things in perspective. That medal would've captured dust. That memory of why I took the selfie and thinking back to my friend and our selfie on that trail run wasn't going anywhere. I was resilient during the race, and I kept things in perspective. I didn't fail, because I scoped out what my empowerment looked like and what my success looked like trying. I did fail to medal, and I was okay with that.

There are numerous times in people's lives when they are fearful to step into the empowerment they own. They fear the next steps ahead, often into unknown territory. This is the place where courage is built. What keeps you from stepping forward? Is it fear of the unknown? Is it the stories you've told yourself about what *could* lie ahead? Is it because of past experiences that you've struggled to recover from? What is different now? Stop and think about that for a moment. If you've worked through this book with the associated action items, take some time to think about what you've examined and the path you are on.

It is a path that involves setting and owning your reality! A path that leads you to choosing to build others up. Footsteps that lead you to courage time and time again because you've made the selfless choice to serve others even when serving yourself may be more enticing and safer. A journey to a regular process that involves investing in others and setting sacred time with yourself for your personal growth investments. The path is one that, in living these choices and honoring others and yourself through them, takes you to a mindset of empowerment and peace in knowing you are owning every step you choose to take. Keep things in perspective when barriers, limiting beliefs, comparisons, judgments, and anything else that tries to tell your ego to jump off this path as quickly as possible come forward. Continue to be resilient and the peace will be there.

Chapter 7
Taking Action with an Acronym

’m not big on small talk, as I confessed in Chapter 4. I like to cut to the chase. It isn't because I don't care about people and what they have to say but instead because I care deeply. I want to get to know you! Whether the topic that's brought us together is business, hobby, faith, or anything else, I want to have meaningful moments with you. I struggle with small talk because I want to get to real talk. What are your passions? What are you doing in life that connects to your purpose? Can I help? One of my favorite pieces of feedback I ever received was from a person at an after-party for an event called the Young Professionals Summit.

I had been given the opportunity to speak at one of the breakout sessions for the event. I had gotten to know some of the attendees over the past year through attending socials hosted by the Young Professionals group. The group was designed for individuals from the ages of twenty-one to forty. I was on the older end, being thirty-five at the time I started attending the socials and getting to know some amazing people. I struggled with the socials at first because I was often approached by people whose first question was "So, what do you do?" I've never been a big fan of this question because I don't want what I do to define me or the person asking the question to decide their response to me from it.

I will often respond to this question with, "Instead of telling you what I do, I'd like to share why I do what I do in all aspects of my life." I then go on to share my purpose to help others grow and develop and inspire them to take action. From my experience with this approach, the conversations seem to take much deeper direction and meaningful relationships grow from them. I don't get to spend time with as many people at the socials, but the quality far outweighs the quantity.

At one of the socials I met an individual and approached him with exploring his purpose. I could tell he was a little nervous and was hesitant to answer. He proceeded to share with me by telling me all the places he'd lived and how it shaped who he was and his purpose. I loved it! I could tell it wasn't rehearsed and was truly genuine. We talked for about thirty minutes and it was such an enjoyable interaction. I, unfortunately, didn't remember to exchange information with him. I went months without seeing him again until the Young Professionals Summit after-party.

I was walking to get a drink when I noticed him at a table, eating alone. I immediately walked over and started to talk with him. At first, he looked a little puzzled, and the story I was telling myself was that he forgot about our interaction. After talking for a few moments, his puzzled look changed.

He said, "Jared, I really appreciate you. I was in one of your sessions today, and I liked what you shared and learned some good pieces." I was listening intently and was not exactly sure where the conversation was going. He continued, "What I liked even more is that you don't just share information you believe is important to helping others; you share it and seem to live it." I was humbled and thankful for this feedback, but what he said next really resonated with me. "I didn't want to come to the event today and actually showed up thirty minutes late because I tried to talk myself out of it this morning. Then I tried to talk myself out of coming to this after-party, but I have been pushing myself to try new things that make me uncomfortable. I haven't seen you for over three months, and I'm amazed that you seem to remember everything we discussed. That means a lot to me. Thank you for making a point to connect. I can tell you care."

I was in awe and so thankful this individual had shared this with me. He was right. I cared about him. I also empathized with him. I love talking with people, but just like him, I had to force myself to be at the after-party. Some call me an introvert with extrovert tendencies. I'm not a big fan of talking with groups in large crowds but truly do love connecting with others, and once I'm engaged, I'm thankful. Working through discomfort in growth can lead to some awesome avenues. He and I went on to talk for about an hour and had another wonderful encounter.

I'll be completely honest. I didn't want to share this story. I didn't like sharing stories like this for a long time because they felt egotistical to me. I didn't want people to think I was trying to toot my own horn or humble brag, as I've heard the term used recently, and I don't share stories like this often. Sometimes, though, I feel it is necessary and no longer fear judgment from others because I'm at peace with myself and my intent and purpose behind sharing a story like this. I shared this story because I wanted to demonstrate that I truly care for others and want to help them. I put a lot of time, effort, and energy into each interaction because of my purpose and knowing that I may be able to impact someone's life in an amazing and growth-filled way, or in a small, piece-of-the-puzzle way. Either way is something to celebrate. I share all this because of what I am going to share next: an acronym.

For a long time, I wasn't a fan of acronyms. I would hear speakers use them on stage or notice writers put them in their work, and they often felt cheesy and forced to me. I was very judgmental in general. It is through my growth and continued effort that my judging has become far less to almost nonexistent, but this is a daily practice. As far as acronyms go, one changed my outlook on them forever and helped me understand that when acronyms aren't forced but built with intent and genuine purpose, they can be an effective tool for growth.

The acronym that inspired my turnaround is BRAVING, created by Dr. Brenè Brown. It is the acronym she has used for a while now to help people dive deeper into understanding trust and using application-based tools to make meaningful changes in their lives and relationships. I am one of those people. The intent and purpose she used with the acronym helped me understand how powerful an acronym can be when it comes with genuineness and heart. Much like my interaction in the story I shared about the man in the Young Professionals group came with full genuineness and heart, this acronym comes with the same intent.

Over time, as I was exploring my work and research helping others become Peaceful Powered Leaders and focusing on the steps in the growth process, I created a powerful and helpful acronym. I offer it as another tool that you can use on a daily basis as a check-in, maybe during your sacred time of reflection, to see where you are in staying PEACEFUL.

P – Peace starts with accountability.

E – Embrace your full spectrum of emotions.

A – Assume positive intent with others.

C – Create kindness opportunities.

E – Empowerment is stepped into, not given.

F – Find your power (to lift others up, to connect, to serve).

U – Understanding should come before answering (Ask questions instead of giving answers).

L – Live your purpose.

Let's examine each letter and the phrase associated with it and how it connects to becoming and growing as a Peaceful Powered Leader.

P – Peace starts with accountability.

Just as the first work of becoming a Peaceful Powered Leader purposefully is being accountable for setting and owning your reality, this first letter of the acronym reminds us we must be accountable to stay in peace. The truth is we own every step we make, every decision we take. If I'm unhappy about something, I have the power to change it or to complain about it. I have the power to work toward a solution that makes me happy or an excuse that makes me frustrated. The accountability is always within my hands.

I once shared this concept with a group of learners, and as we explored scenarios for about twenty minutes to test this theory, one person shouted out, "That's it! You've taken the power of excuses away from me." I asked the learner what she meant by this. She stated, "I get it. I always have a choice, and if I want to be accountable, I must realize I own that choice, regardless of the circumstances, because both ideal and nonideal circumstances are a part of life." This learner was correct and went on to accomplish some pretty amazing things in her life as she put this learning into her thought process and action. Peace is ours to own and it starts with our accountability.

If you are struggling with a situation, and are grasping for a starting point, think about how you can center yourself with the question, "What can I do with the situation I am in right now?" Think about that question for a moment and the power it has. You have the ability to step into scoping what is currently within your control and what you have the ability to influence. It is your choice! It allows you to move forward toward possible solutions. You can quickly step out of a mindset of waiting, which often carries with it unrest, into a mindset of action. You have to be accountable to this and when you are struggling with your peace, the starting point can always come back to, "How can I be accountable right now and own this reality?" You've got this!

E - Embrace your full spectrum of emotions.

We explored how important it is to be aware of all of our emotions and not view them as positive or negative but instead as easier and more difficult to embrace. They don't have to be simply defined as good or bad because our emotions are more complex than that. In our effort to be a Peaceful Powered Leader, we must be accountable for our emotions and learn how to embrace the easy ones *and* the more difficult ones.

We aren't going to be happy all the time or positive all the time. Life doesn't work that way but becoming more comfortable embracing when we aren't will help us become more and more proficient at working our way back to the emotions we want to embrace consistently.

I remember an experience with emotions I learned a great deal from. It was a moment that, for a while, I wish I could have taken back, erased, but after I reflected and grew from it, it became a key learning for me. I was sitting at my desk on a Friday afternoon, finishing up a few items before heading home for a fun Friday night out with family when two team members walked in. One team member said, "We need to share with you an experience we had this afternoon." The team members proceeded to tell me how they had been berated in a training they were facilitating. I could see one of the team members was visibly shaken by the experience. The other team member shared how a particular leader, who had a reputation for leaning toward the pessimistic view and for often publicly sharing criticisms, had "gone off" on the two of them in the training session. As I heard this, without asking myself, "What would accountability look like from me as a leader right now?" I jumped into emotion and judgment. Because this leader had a reputation for "giving people a hard time and lacking respect," I didn't try to sort facts from fiction or to separate out my team members' emotions or to refrain from the kind of storytelling in which I supplied details. I simply went to judgment.

I proceeded to listen to the two members who were upset. I didn't ask a lot of questions, and as I heard them describe the situation, I could feel my emotions start to take over. I thought about other instances when people had described similar situations with this leader to me. The two team members shared that other leaders came up after the session was over and apologized for the way this leader had acted. Hearing this only led me to feel I needed to "stick up" for my team and that the emotions I felt were even more validated. I thanked them for sharing and for completing the training. I shared I would address the situation with the leader.

After the conversation ended, I went back to my computer and found that I already had an email from this leader. It was a straightforward email that asked some pretty basic questions. However, my emotions were in full swing! Instead of responding to the email, I responded to the emotions I was having. I most certainly was drawn away from peace in that moment, but I told myself that I was serving my two team members. I didn't take time to reflect on my current state or to address my emotions properly so I could approach the situation by checking facts, seeking to understand, and leveraging separate realities. Instead, I responded to the email with the story I had heard combined with the story I was telling myself. Before I knew it, the email exchange had escalated, and I told the leader I would like to talk face to face the following week about the matter.

The meeting came and, as one would probably imagine, it did not get off to a great start. By the time of the meeting, I had reflected and realized I failed to do some pretty important things before addressing the leader in the email. I failed to assume positive intent for all involved and work to leverage separate realties. I failed to assess my emotions and how I could embrace them while searching for facts instead of reacting to what was shared with me. I trusted the two team members who shared their experience with me, but I also needed to remember that they may have brought emotions into the situation. I also needed to remember that the leader may not have acted in the most appropriate manner in the training, but that doesn't mean she wasn't trying her best that day. I needed to seek to understand how my emotions were coming forward and then seek to understand where all parties were coming from and what were the facts versus what was storytelling that emotions were driving. This would have kept me in a greater level of peace and opened the door to a better conversation and interaction with the leader, instead of the conversation I did have in the meeting, which involved a lot of defensiveness from all the parties. As the meeting continued, I realized I could've embraced my emotions in a much better way. While the experience in the moment wasn't comfortable, the reflection and learning afterward were so vital. Part of embracing our full spectrum of emotions is learning from our missteps. The goal isn't to be perfect, but to make progress and be more aware of when our emotions are taking over. Eventually this leads to us addressing our emotions appropriately when we find ourselves in them.

Don't ignore emotions. Work to reflect on what emotions you are comfortable feeling and responding to. What are the emotions that you are less comfortable engaging in? How can you be deliberate in trying to embrace those emotions that are harder for you currently? What would progress look like? What goal(s) would you like to set around emotions to correlate to your growth and remaining in peace as you power forward as a leader?

A - Assume positive intent.

Oh, the stories I could tell about the storytelling I've done in my life could make up some interesting novels! I was a great storyteller, meaning I often didn't assume positive intent when it came to others but instead mixed fact with fiction in many circumstances. If someone gave me feedback that was hard to hear, I didn't think, "This person wants me to succeed and this is their way of helping me." Nope! Instead, I often thought, "This person clearly is out to try and make me fail, and this feedback is their way of putting me down." That was a much more common narrative for me. I had to work on changing that narrative, and through the process, I became a much happier and more peaceful person.

I started to stick to facts and ask myself: "What do I know for sure?" and "Is this a story I am making up or is it rooted in facts?" As I started to ask myself these questions, my thought process shifted. I stuck to facts and assumed positive intent in others. Some would challenge me on this process as being naïve. My respectful challenge back was, "Can you prove otherwise?" When I'd ask that question, people would sometimes share a track record of the person I was assuming positive intent about. I would acknowledge that while the track record they shared may be accurate, for the situation I was in with this person or that person, I was sticking to the facts of what I knew for sure. It kept me out of drama and in much more happiness in all areas of my life. It also had a byproduct of developing some amazing relationships with others because I opened the door to a different relationship than some had experienced before.

Let me also be clear—assuming positive intent with others doesn't mean I don't also have healthy boundaries in place to continue to build trust as well. Those boundaries were based on fact, though, not fiction. With the assumption of positive intent, it also becomes much easier to give grace to others. This practice helps root individuals in peace, not contempt.

C – Create kindness opportunities.

Imagine what the world would be like if we were all just 10 percent kinder every day. Don't continue to read just yet—really imagine! Opportunities to be kind are around us every single day. We just have to be accountable to look for them, step into the opportunity, take hold of it, and act on it. That's it! So often we miss out because of the stories we tell ourselves: "I'm too busy to help" or "That won't really make an impact or difference." Now imagine if we changed our minds and took just 10 percent more of the opportunities we have to act in kindness. What could happen? What could spread? At a minimum, we made an impact for someone else and, at a maximum, we could be the example that changes the world.

A good place to start researching kindness is by checking out Orly Wahba's TED Talk. I promise you won't be disappointed. I currently don't know Orly at all, but her story and purpose have helped change my life and the way I view kindness and look for opportunities to create it for others and myself. Being kind to others connects right into being a Peaceful Powered Leader through building others up, taking the opportunity to put service to others ahead of service to self, and investing in others.

Additionally, challenge yourself to examine barriers to your kindness. I grew up with an influential person in my life regularly reminding me to be careful of others. "People will take advantage of your kindness; make sure you are getting something in return" was the message shared over and over with me. I realized this experience was a barrier to my kindness. I was kind to others, but I was keeping tabs on my kindness with others. This process didn't open the door for full kindness and often kept me away from peace because I was concerned with the "score" remaining balanced in relationships with others. As I explored this barrier, I realized I had to address how I viewed trust for me personally. I acknowledged it was important to have healthy boundaries and to be able to say "no" or "not now" at times, but it was also important to let go of the thought process that a "score" was needed. I started to shift my expectations of others and challenge myself to examine my motive: "Am I doing this because I can and want to be fully kind, without any expectations from this person or group?" If the answer was yes, then I jumped into the experience. If the answer was no, I explored why. If it was because of a healthy boundary, I was able to stay in peace. If it was because of past barriers or limiting beliefs, I worked to grow and progress past or through them in order to continue to be able to create kindness opportunities or take part in acts of kindness.

E – Empowerment is stepped into, not given.

This piece flows right into how Peaceful Powered Leaders empower themselves and create an environment for others to succeed. Empowerment connects to accountability. I have accomplished so many things because I simply tried. They were things people said, "You can't do that in this organization; you'll get in trouble." Guess what? I did it, didn't get in trouble, and many times, I got rewarded for being willing to try and for the accomplishments that came from that trying. Sometimes others would say I was bold as a leader, but the truth was, I stuck to my values and simply stepped into the empowerment that was in front of me. It wasn't given to me; I had to be willing to try, and sometimes that meant failure too. Trying, though, allowed me to be at peace with myself and the decisions I had made.

Unfortunately, I spent a lot of years out of peace because I wasn't willing to step into empowerment. I've reflected on some of these times and want to share them to lend perspective and potential reflection to you in thinking about your own life.

One instance took me back to childhood as a twelve-year-old. I remember sweat dripping off my head as I sat up against the large pecan tree in southern Georgia outside our home. That tree had a wooden backboard and metal basketball goal attached to it. I spent countless hours around that tree. Some of those hours were spent with my father, others were spent with neighborhood kids, while many were spent alone. Each hour was practice for becoming an NBA star! I had dreams of playing in the NBA, and as a five-foot, ten-inch twelve-year-old, I thought I had a shot. I was much taller than the other kids my age and thought I'd keep growing. I loved the sport. Unfortunately, by the time I ended my sophomore season in high school, I was the same size, and when people told me I wouldn't grow anymore and that the NBA was a pipe dream, I listened. I let height be the excuse to embrace my limiting beliefs and lost sight of the practice, effort, and growth goals. I transitioned from practicing basketball regularly to only playing pick-up games for fun. I let that dream go, instead of stepping into the empowerment I owned. Still today, I watch NBA games in person and on television with so much passion for the sport and respect for the people who play it professionally. I know the work, time, energy, and effort they put in to get there. They stayed in the empowerment and didn't listen to the limiting beliefs I'm sure came their way time and time again.

The very next year, I found a new dream! I auditioned for the fall high school play. It was a musical. I hadn't sung before, but I found I had the ability to be coached (I learned this through basketball), and I could also imitate. I knew nothing about singing, but as the drama director asked me to sing certain ways in the audition, I found I was able to, and I obtained a lead role in the play. I loved being on stage and was in every play performed at my high school through graduation. I won acting awards both junior and senior year of high school. I dreamt about becoming an actor. The dream wasn't as far off as the NBA dream from my perspective either. I had the opportunity to talk with a Broadway producer. As I shared my interests, he asked me, "Could I give you a piece of advice?" I excitedly said yes. He proceeded, "If you can do anything else, do it! The world of acting is full of heartbreak. It is a tough life and unless it is the absolute, only thing you want to do in life, do something else." Guess what, I listened. For the second time, I listened to others and walked away from my dreams and the empowerment I owned. I let the limits of others impact me and I put limits on myself.

For years, I continued the process of listening to other people's limits about me, and I put limits on myself. I didn't think I was good enough and struggled with my peace. I told myself I wasn't good enough to graduate college. I told myself I wasn't good enough to write a book, stand on a stage in front of large groups, be a certified coach who people would pay to partner with, and the list goes on. I put limits on myself and listened to the limits that others put on me. Then, I had a conversation with someone who challenged me. I didn't know this person too well except for interactions at professional events and brief interactions at church. She asked to have lunch.

While at lunch, she shared her goals with me. It was refreshing to hear her goals and dreams and clear plans she had to obtain them. She then asked me about my dreams and goals. As I started to share, she challenged me. She pushed back and said, "Jared, I've watched you on a stage. I've heard how you lead others. I've seen how you connect passionately in the work you do. Why are your dreams and goals so limited? Why do you not believe you can be on the same stage with those you admire?" Her challenge was a wakeup call because I had no answer for her. I realized in my mind I had put limits on myself. I had decided I wasn't good enough and didn't choose to step into the empowerment right in front of me.

I couldn't push aside these limiting beliefs overnight, but I worked on a plan to challenge myself any time I felt I was limiting myself. I also held myself accountable to not let others' limiting beliefs be placed on me. And guess what? Amazing things started to happen, and I was finding more and more of the peace we've explored together in this book. I started to really dream again. I started to see my next book on bookshelves in national bookstores, living my intent to inspire others toward action with the learnings in it. I started to see my name advertised as a keynote on the national learning events I have been attending for years. I started to reach out to people who were on my admiration list because they had already done these things to see if I could partner with them in different ways or learn directly from them. Many of them responded, and I am partnering now with some in powerful ways that are bringing my dreams closer to reality every day and providing new options to help others grow and develop. It's been less than two years since I shed my limiting beliefs and the gap between my dreams and reality is becoming smaller and smaller each day. Make no mistake, though, this takes work each and every day toward improvement and progress.

As Malcolm Gladwell shared in his book, *Outliers: The Story of Success*, his research has shown that with 10,000 hours of practice a person can become a master performer in a given field. I saw the truth of this so many times in my life. I saw how much skill I gained when I entered my freshman year of basketball. I was good, on my way to great, and it had nothing to do with my height. I put limiting beliefs on myself, though, instead of empowerment ownership. I remember hearing from a person, who is now a film producer, how much my acting had improved by one of my last performances and what I could do if I continued to explore the field, but I put limits on myself. I now can stand on a stage and connect with each person in the room on topics I'm passionate about. Not because I have a knack for speaking, but because I've spent 10,000 hours researching, exploring, and practicing in this field, combined with a heart and passion to help others. My passion has connected to my purpose and the empowerment I've given myself.

When Dr. Brenè Brown put a call out to leadership and organizational development practitioners to become certified facilitators for one of her programs, I was so excited. As I read through the requirements, I realized I met each one. It was a defining moment for me. They all involved hours upon hours of work in formal education, practitioner work, certification work, and application. I didn't get accepted into the program because I was lucky. I got accepted because I put the work in for years and years prior to the call, in spite of my limiting beliefs during some of those years. I am thankful because the work has helped me grow into a different kind of father, husband, friend, coach, team member, leader, and more.

Take some time whenever you feel yourself out of peace and reflect on where limiting beliefs may be causing you to venture from empowerment and not dream your biggest dreams and live the life you know you are capable of. It is such a powerful process if you work toward being consistent and putting in practices that help you catch when limiting beliefs come your way and keep you out of peace.

F – Find your power.

So often power is given associated descriptors that make it seem as though it is on this pedestal we can't get to. But power, from my experience, is easy to jump into when our intent is in the right place. Power could be giving our time to someone who needs help. I can't tell you how many free coaching sessions I've given people as a certified coach. I have experience and I could seek something from those sessions, but I don't. My purpose in life is to help others grow and develop and inspire them to take action and, with that purpose, I have the power to impact. Reflect on where your power lies and how you can use it to serve someone, to help them, or to simply connect with them because they are lonely and want a friend.

Have you ever taken time to reflect on what your power is? I remember a moment with a peer leader years ago that caused me to reflect on this question. The topic of titles was on the table. The organization was going through some restructures, and there was discussion around changing titles. As the conversation developed, one leader shared that they didn't think titles were a big deal and as quickly as they said the comment, I saw a big shift in body language from another person in the room. The individual sat forward in their chair. They, with intensity, pulled their badge off of their shirt and put it out in front of them, in the direction of the leader who just shared they didn't believe titles were a big deal. The individual said firmly, with badge in hand, "You see this title right here. No one listened to me until I had that title. That title gave me the power I needed to make change in this organization. That title is a very big deal. That title is also my power." The conversation went on for a while but eventually shifted to the fact that the organization may have a larger culture problem if titles are what give leaders a voice. What comes to mind when you think of power? Is it associated with a title? Why is this? Can you change this? I believe so. Titles may be important, but they aren't the root of our powers.

I have the title of father that was given to me when my son was born. The title, however, doesn't mean much to my son, and there are a lot of individuals who play a parental role in someone's life without bearing a title. It is not the title that makes our relationship special with those people. It is not my superpower with my son.

My superpower for my son, I believe, is that I spend time connecting with him. I spend time swimming with him, which he loves. We take exciting journeys together on road trips to wrestling events, which transitioned to comic conventions, and I imagine will morph into other things over time. At the root of it all, my superpower with him, and with so many others, is connectedness.

I find I am able to help others in so many ways when I focus on my power of connectedness, and I am also very peaceful when I am in connectedness. There have been times when I've worked to partner with someone and things just weren't gelling. I will often take a step back and try to evaluate what I could do differently to help. Time and time again, when reviewing what is missing, I realize I am not truly using my power to connect. I work to flex my communication style to connect in genuine ways and, before I know it, we are gelling. It doesn't happen by chance. It happens because I know my power and I use it. It has nothing to do with a title. It wasn't given to me. It was something I worked at and continue to work at and progress. When we know our power and carry positive intent in how we use it, some productive things can happen that are often followed by a great sense of peace.

U – Understanding should come before answering.

As a Peaceful Powered Leader, it is hard to serve others if we are telling instead of listening. The truly wise look for opportunities to learn and fully understand before answering a question or giving an insight. Often, the truly powerful don't give answers but instead ask questions. They ask questions to help others seek understanding because they understand each path is unique and each purpose is different. A large reason why Peaceful Powered Leaders set sacred time with themselves is to reflect and seek to understand. When we let go of fear of judgment and step into a mindset of learning, we look to understand in ways that are important to us, instead of ways that may show us in a certain light to others.

Understanding takes time. It takes the ability to listen for what may be being said without it actually being said. How often have you partaken in a conversation and early into the conversation you found yourself wanting to speak and no longer being fully present listening? I know I have done that time and time again. I often find out later that my anticipation to speak, instead of understand, caused me to miss out on key points. It also hindered my ability to ensure the person in front of me felt like I was there to serve them or others versus serving myself. When we understand, it becomes easier in many instances to connect what is being said to a purpose. A purpose we can relate to, connect with, or help move forward in a more genuine way. Seeking to understand is also seeking to care. When we find ourselves struggling to find our peace, we should ask whether we have worked to fully understand what is in front of us. If not, what do we need to seek out, listen to, and work to understand to get there?

L – Live your purpose.

Our purpose can be a driving force to serve others, build others up, invest in ourselves, set an environment of empowerment, and so much more. Our purpose is our why in life. It helps us see through the smoke and mirrors of the what in life, things like title or status that we hustle to attain and maintain and that often keep us from peace. Our purpose is our guiding light, and when we have strong connection to our values, it becomes easier and easier to live our purpose and have it powered by peace. Ensure you stay connected to your purpose and set sacred time with yourself as a consistent way to check in on the connection and how you are living your purpose.

Finding the acronym PEACEFUL wasn't a forced exercise for me. It came about through learning from my own research and experience, as well as that of many leaders I've had the pleasure to connect with. I encourage you to use it as a centering tool any time you may find yourself out of alignment with one or more of the principles of being a Peaceful Powered Leader. Remember to start in order, because what I've discovered more often than not is that when our peace is out of alignment, it is because our accountability isn't where we need it to be. And you now know, we have full control to change that.

Chapter 8
Staying in Peace in the Midst of Uncertainty

As I write this chapter, our world is currently in the midst of what so many have called an unprecedented time—the global pandemic of COVID-19—and with it has come great uncertainty. For me, the pandemic has also brought a new test of each component of being a Peaceful Powered Leader. I wondered if all these elements, which were effective in normal times, would deliver the same results when the rubber went beyond simply meeting the road and instead had to run for miles upon miles over rough terrain. Would the practices for becoming a Peaceful Powered Leader hold up to the wear and tear?

The closest I ever came to experiencing a time like the pandemic was going through Hurricane Katrina. My wife and I sheltered at the air force base I worked on just a little over a quarter mile from the Gulf Coast as the massive force came ashore. We lost our home, vehicles, and almost all our possessions in that storm. There was death and destruction all along the coast. We felt tremendous uncertainty, as did everyone around us. I hoped to never endure something like it again.

Today, what I witnessed during Katrina in a very small portion of the world is occurring on a global level. That is hard to accept. During the pandemic, I strive to be empathetic to everyone's journey, which is unique and different for each of us. My experience of Hurricane Katrina contributed to making me an adult educator and coach who tries to help others develop by providing true sustenance. I always work to ensure my teachings aren't just good in theory but hold up in the real world. However, if the results are real, that means achieving them often involves hard work, as well as accepting a level of rawness, of truth speaking. Over the years, people who attend my workshops often comment on this quality in my coaching. They give feedback like, "I related to what you were saying because you didn't sugarcoat it. You provided real-life examples that I could tell you'd been through and had used these tools. You were vulnerable and showed that you, too, failed at times and knew this stuff was hard, but that it worked." Those comments resonate with me each time they are shared. They are a gut check that I am in touch with reality and fully living my purpose. I don't practice theory; I practice reality, and reality is messy. It takes discipline, time, and action to make changes. I also practice optimism. I acknowledge the reality we are in is very tough. I also acknowledge that we can take actions to make the future better. Our reality can shift over time as we work to grow and see results, which increases our optimism. These tools for becoming a Peaceful Powered Leader work, if you put in the effort to understand them and then actively choose to apply them. They are working for me right now in this unprecedented time.

I recently had a person reach out to me through text with something that they appeared not to be happy about. They felt I had taken an approach in trying to live my purpose in one area that wasn't agreeable to them. I was thrown off for a moment when I first read the text, as the person appeared to ignore some vital points previously discussed, and I started to judge. I then stopped, and said, "What would peace for me look like right now?" I answered myself, "Peace would be to assume positive intent with this person." It was a person I had known for quite some time and respected. I wanted to respond to the text by defending my views and approach. I stopped though and said to myself, "If I am assuming positive intent and wanting to stay in peace, what would be the accountable approach?" Aha, what was that? It was the first step in being a Peaceful Powered Leader. I was owning my reality and being accountable. The reality was this person was upset, and I wanted to first be right. I decided I wanted to be in peace instead. I didn't want to judge, because I wasn't then, nor have I ever been, in a place to judge. I don't know that person's journey. When I decided to stay in peace, that judgment quickly faded, and I said to myself, "This doesn't seem characteristic of this person 90 percent of the time. This person may be dealing with something tough right now, and this message was their best today. I can accept that and move forward in peace." I stayed accountable to where I wanted to be. I replied to the person with a few short words and thanked them for sharing their insights with me. I was not right or the hero; they were not wrong or the villain. We were just two people trying to do our best. In years past, I would have done my best to prove I was right or I would have needed to work to ensure the person wasn't upset with me. I would've lost sleep over the situation. I would've wrestled back and forth in an effort to prove. I don't prove anymore; I live. I live in peace and strive to help others grow and develop so that they may inspire those they lead to take action toward what they truly want to achieve.

A funny thing happened just a day or two after that challenging text came in. I received another text. It was from a person I had coached letting me know her family was okay and that amidst everything occurring with COVID-19, she had taken on a new role. It was a promotion. She thanked me for helping her as her coach and taking time to invest in her. This was a person I had the pleasure to meet when she was only a few months into her formal leadership journey, but it was obvious even then that she had been leading for a long time. She was eager to grow and learn and understood the importance of investing in herself and others. I could see she already had been living as a Peaceful Powered Leader. She set and owned her reality. She received opportunity after opportunity, but she didn't jump at each one. Instead, she evaluated how the offered change would impact her, her reality, those she led, and whether it was aligned with her entire life. I also watched her respect-fully challenge executives when it came to serving those she led. She shared that this wasn't easy to do, and she worried at times how speak-ing up would impact her career, but she knew it was the right thing to do and it ultimately allowed her to stay connected to her values and the peace that came with that action. She was serving others in lieu of serving herself. I share about her because there is one truth that I didn't highlight in this book that is so important—Peaceful Powered Leaders power each other. Her courage, willingness to be accountable, commit-ment to building others up and investing in them, and encouragement of others to step into the empowerment they own are always reminders for me—reminders of living our values but also that the journey to peace and staying there isn't always easy. Peaceful Powered Leaders understand that together is better. They help each other in the easy and tough times. They remind each other of the optimism they bring into the world. Optimism, for me, means being intentional in remembering that we can bring hope about the future. It doesn't mean simply saying, "Let's focus on positivity and have a glass-half-full approach" but in-stead means being active in bringing that optimism to life in how we connect, what we do, and why we do it.

While I didn't share the challenging text I had recently received or how powerful her text was for me in that moment, I did express my gratitude for her contacting me and describing the impact I had in her career. I told her how excited I was for her to have this new role. Her reaching out was a reminder of my purpose and the importance of striving to bring my best in living as a Peaceful Powered Leader. It was a reminder that being a Peaceful Powered Leader doesn't simply lie in the decent, good, or great moments only but also in the gritty, gut-wrenching, sad, frustrating moments. Our true test of peace often will come more in those latter more difficult moments than in the mo-ments that are easier and more ideal for us. To live in and stay in that peace, come what may, takes practice. It involves continual growth as we step into new experiences and encounter new challenges.

As I worked through identifying the components of becoming a Peaceful Powered Leader, I was deliberate in avoiding descriptions of what a Peaceful Powered Leader wasn't. I struggled at times to resist this approach—like "How *not* to invest in others"—but for the most part, I was able to steer clear. I wanted you, the reader, the learner, the person engaging in this growth opportunity, to stay focused on you. Many times, I've seen ego creep occur, along with judgment and comparison, when we explore what something doesn't look like. We hear an example that makes us cringe, and we, often unintentionally, think about someone we know who has done this cringe-worthy example. We drift away, we compare, and we lose focus.

In the midst of this unprecedented time, I am seeing some of those cringe-worthy examples, but I am also seeing the Peaceful Powered Leaders truly rise. My family has yet to be affected by the health effects of COVID-19, but as someone who has worked in healthcare systems for over a decade now, I see the impact it is having on so many in various ways. During the days leading up to the state-mandated stay-at-home orders and into the weeks of the mandate being in effect, the mindset of staying in peace was tested time and time again.

Living life as a Peaceful Powered Leader involves regularly connecting deliberately in all six areas we have discussed. It is a sequential and revolving process, and it is hard to go to steps two through six if you aren't fully embracing the first, the true foundation: setting and owning your reality. This keeps the ego in check and keeps us out of comparison, judgment, shame, fear of the what-ifs, and many other unpeaceful thoughts. It doesn't mean as a Peaceful Powered Leader we won't go to those places, but as we put the actionable work in, if we do go there, it should become easier for us to get back to where we want to be in healthy ways. This process also keeps us closely connected to our values. It reminds us why we are building others up, how we are serving others and investing in them, the importance of sacred time with ourselves, and how the pieces ultimately lead us to being able to scope empowerment for others and ensure we are stepping into the empowerment provided to us.

The exercises were intended to be thought-provoking and lead you to sources for next steps in your growth. Reading some of the literature will open the door to further learning and building on the foundation you've started here. Working with a coach will help in crafting ongoing action plans that can lead to new levels of awareness and understanding. It is your choice to stay in the peace you own, the emotions that come with it, and the continuous building you desire to do.

Experiences will happen in your life that will challenge your peace. Standing up for what you believe to be right in service of taking care of those you lead can have consequences and could even leave you without employment for a time. It is hard to stay in peace when something like this happens. It should be even harder to compromise your values, though. Keep this in mind during these difficult moments. Connecting with other human beings can be hard at times. We all have emotions, and our emotions can sometimes lead us away from the truth or reality in situations. Emotions aren't positive or negative; they are easier and harder to embrace. I'm of the belief that all emotions can benefit us with their potential to spur growth, as long as we work to embrace them in healthy ways.

As I was writing this book, I grew and evolved in my understanding of peace. I am much closer to my faith value than I was when I started. I'm still not there all day, every day. I am a human with imperfections. This doesn't mean I'm not okay or good enough. It just means I continue to be a work in progress, and I need to remember this about others too. My peace continues to evolve as I evolve. It is, however, still centered on the six components of being a Peaceful Powered Leader, which keep my growth moving forward with strong intensity in these very uncertain times. I'm sharing this right now because I wouldn't have been able to share it the day I started working on this book. My peace has been tested in new ways, and if we are truly working to grow and evolve, our peace will grow and evolve as well. I once heard an author share (unfortunately I don't recall who) that a book they wrote was like an old friend. It represented a moment in time for them, which was a joy to go back and visit as a reminder of the journey to that friend and the journey since last seeing that friend. If we are truly growing and evolving, this should be true of our peace and our development path. We may look back on that friend and be thankful for our time with them but also celebrate where we are today, how we've grown, and the true effort we put in along the way.

Being a Peaceful Powered Leader is far from being perfect. Life is messy, and unexpected situations arise all the time. That includes work, family, friends, and every other beautiful relationship, even with ourselves. While it is messy, it is our reality to own. We get to choose what we put out into the world and how we connect to others in it. We could decide to embrace our emotions and work through them because we aren't always going to be happy, and that is okay.

Embrace all emotions, and if you are living the pieces that power peaceful leaders, you will have tools to grow from embracing them. There isn't a secret formula, but there are a few things that take work and work well. I don't know about you, but I want my life and this book to be about helping others. It may go under the self-help section in the bookstore, but as Simon Sinek, the author of *Start with Why*, *Leaders Eat Last*, and *The Infinite Game*, has shared more than once, I'd rather my book go under the helping-others section. It doesn't exist in most bookstores, but the Peaceful Powered Leaders know it is there.

Encourage courage, inspire action, and spread kindness! It is your choice, your opportunity to step into. Embrace it, own all parts of it, and keep connecting. I'm waiting to hear from you and ready to invest. Be well my friends and own your peace.

Ready for Next Steps?

A re you looking for continued growth and development on your journey as a Peaceful Powered Leader? Connect with Jared today to discuss coaching, speaking, and workshop options for your organization and you.

Jared has spoken at conferences and client events around the globe with engaging keynotes tailor-made for today's leaders at events including:

- Association and Industry Conferences
- Annual Meetings
- Company Functions
- Leadership, Executive, and Board Retreats
- Onsite Coaching and Consulting
- Client Engagements

You can connect directly with Jared at PeacefulPoweredLeadership. com. While there, you can gain access to coaching videos, resources and exercises, and a community of leaders striving to create workplaces that encourage courage, inspire action, and spread kindness.

Acknowledgments

The lesson I hold dearest, that was so wonderfully learned in my years of leadership development, is we are truly better together. Peaceful Powered Leadership was born out of connectedness and writing this book wouldn't have been possible without my community. The following words are for them.

To my family

To my spouse, Nichole, and son, Cayden, for always being onboard to listen to a new idea and share the energy and excitement you know brainstorming and connecting with others brings me. Our journey together gets more and more exciting each year, and you've always allowed me to pursue my dreams even when it caused a shift in our life. Thank you.

To my mother and father for always being a huge cheering section. You don't always know exactly what it is I'm doing, but you know it brings me joy and you've always supported it through questions, insights, and celebrations.

To my brother for seeing my growth over the years and leaning in to connect and grow together.

The unwavering support and love from you all truly mean the world to me.

To my friends who became family

To Jake, for being the epitome of a Peaceful Powered Leader and showing me how passionate and appreciative someone can be about learning and growing. We've been on a journey that has led to a friendship I cherish. The way you treat others, the care you take for each person you encounter, has been a wonderful example to watch. You taught me the importance of presence and how to cherish our time in the moment.

To Sarah B., for helping me see the only limitations one has is what they decide themselves. You saw my opportunities to achieve my dreams well before I ever did and ensured I knew I was capable. Thank you for supporting, not judging, each step of the way.

To Loni, for reminding me to always have fun on the journey. You helped me understand grit in a new way. I admire your ability to pick people up and show them how to dust themselves off when tough times arise while continuing to support them throughout the process.

To Chris, for being my reading partner and sharing the love of research and exploration with me. You reminded me time and time again of the power of checking in on others and the impact of small moments of engagement.

To Sarah H., for explaining to me what courage was long before I fully understood it. You continuously helped me see that the workplace could be both professional and humanistic together, both serious and fun, and both engaging and entertaining. Thank you for the laughs and lessons during a time I was searching for the next path on my journey.

To Jason, for helping me embrace curiosity in so many different ways. Your level of care for others and the way you embrace exploration, not judgement, with others has been a guiding example. Thank you for your kindness and the door you opened to fellowship.

To the supporters and team members

To Tori, Jamie, Jason, Kara, and Bryan, for not only believing in the words of this book but also believing in my purpose and opening the door to partner with your teams in an active effort to continue to grow Peaceful Powered Leaders. Each of you brought forward amazing support to help invest further in the lives of those you lead, and I am truly grateful.

To Cy Wakeman, who has been a mentor and guiding example for me over the years. From her time writing the foreword to this book to allowing me to interview her and her support at every step of my journey, she has made an everlasting impact. A shoutout to her amazing team who have always been so kind and supportive too.

To Kristen Hadeed, Nataly Kogan, and David Shove-Brown for graciously providing time for me to interview you. Each of you brings so much joy and light into this world. I smile each time I see your faces, whether in person, virtually, or on a post. Thank you for the example you set as leaders.

To the entire team at Morgan James. Their belief in this book, and partnership in making it happen, is truly an incredible gift.

Lastly, you don't need a title to lead; I have had some titles that designated me as a formal leader though. I will never forget each person on those teams I had the privilege to serve. It was nothing short of a true honor to collaborate and partner with each of you. I'm so thankful for the many of you who had grace with me as I often made mistakes and missteps. What I am so thankful for is still being in contact with so many of you and seeing how each of you has continued to invest in yourself and others and build others up both as informal and formal leaders.

About The Author

Jared Narlock is a speaker and talent development coach with more than 16 years of experience partnering with C-level executives, Chief Culture Officers, Leaders, and HR professionals on how to engage and develop those they have the privilege to serve. His background encompasses all aspects of Human Resources, with emphasis in organizational development and employee relations. Jared is a former Vice

President of Talent Development and Director of People and Organizational Development, TEDx speaker, and his writings have been published on Forbes.com and TrainingIndustry.com. He's a regular guest on development and growth podcasts and posts weekly on his blog, The Peaceful Powered Way. After finishing his graduate degree, Jared went on to further his passion for learning and serving others by obtaining certifications with the International Coach Federation as an Associate Certified Coach and with the Society for Human Resource Management as a Senior Certified Professional. He is a veteran of the United States Air Force and currently resides with his wife and son in Orlando, FL.

Endnotes

1   Adkins, A., and Rigoni, B. (2016, June 30). Millennials want jobs to be development opportunities. Gallup. Retrieved from https://www.gallup.com/workplace/236438/millennials-jobs-development-opportunities.aspx

2   Kogan, N. (n.d.). The happier method. Happier. Retrieved from https://www.happier.com/the-happier-method/

3   Ong, A. D., Benson, L., Zautra, A. J., and Ram, N. (2018). Emo-diversity and biomarkers of inflammation. Emotion, 18(1), 3–14. Retrieved from https://www.apa.org/pubs/journals/releases/emo-emo0000343.pdf

4   Robertson, C., (n.d.). How gratitude can change your life. Rick Hanson. Retrieved from https://www.rickhanson.net/how-gratitude-can-change-your-life/

5   Carpenter, D. (n.d.). The science behind gratitude (and how it can change your life). Happify Daily. Retrieved from https://www.happify.com/hd/the-science-behind-gratitude/

6   Korb, A. (2012, November 20). The grateful brain: The neuroscience of giving thanks. Psychology Today. Retrieved from https://www.psychologytoday.com/us/blog/prefrontal-nudity/201211/the-grateful-brain

7   Porter, J. (March 21, 2017). Why you should make time for self-reflection (Even if you hate doing it). Harvard Business Review. Retrieved from https://hbr.org/2017/03/why-you-should-make-time-for-self-reflection-even-if-you-hate-doing-it

8   Porter, J. (March 21, 2017). Why you should make time for self-reflection (Even if you hate doing it). Harvard Business Review. Retrieved from https://hbr.org/2017/03/why-you-should-make-time-for-self-reflection-

even-if-you-hate-doing-it

9   Vasel, K. (2014, June 24). How you're spending most of your time. CNN. Retrieved from https://money.cnn.com/2015/06/24/pf/time-use-survey/index.html

10   LinkedIn. (2018). Workplace learning report: The rise and responsibility of talent development in the new labor market. LinkedIn Learning. Retrieved from https://learning.linkedin.com/resources/workplace-learning-report-2018

A free ebook edition
is available with the
purchase of this book.

To claim your free ebook edition:

1. Visit MorganJamesBOGO.com
2. Sign your name CLEARLY in the space
3. Complete the form and submit a photo of the entire copyright page
4. You or your friend can download the ebook to your preferred device

Morgan James
BOGO™

A **FREE** ebook edition is available for you
or a friend with the purchase of this print book.

CLEARLY SIGN YOUR NAME ABOVE

Instructions to claim your free ebook edition:
1. Visit MorganJamesBOGO.com
2. Sign your name CLEARLY in the space above
3. Complete the form and submit a photo
   of this entire page
4. You or your friend can download the ebook
   to your preferred device

Print & Digital Together Forever.

Snap a photo

Free ebook

Read anywhere